REGRESSION ANALYSIS IN EDUCATIONAL RESEARCH

By
John D. Williams
University of North Dakota

MSS Information Corporation
655 Madison Avenue, New York, N. Y. 10

CONTENTS

PREFACE

This short text is unusual in several respects, particularly as it applies to its intended audience (student-researchers and practicing educational researchers). An assumption is made throughout that the reader has access to a computer; it is not necessary to be a programmer, however, as a single multiple purpose multiple regression program will execute almost all the techniques employed. The specific approach used here is always oriented toward the unsophisticated reader. Thus, a deliberate attempt has been made to use the simplest solution to the problem at hand.

The intent here is to "hook" the reader on the use of regression as a problem solving technique so that the researcher can focus on his research problems rather than become totally wound up in a confusing data analysis.

CHAPTER ONE

INTRODUCTION

1.1 Beginning the Study of Regression

At the onset, it is best to be frank. First, it is assumed that the reader has at least been exposed to a first course in statistics that included, among other things, coverage for correlation, regression and the t test. Hopefully, it also included something on the analysis of variance. In one sense, this minimal requirement would be ignored as these topics are covered, from a regression viewpoint, in the present text. On the other hand, some background in "traditional: statistics is worthwhile for several reasons. First, most researchers, particularly those researchers who have a minimal background in statistics, will talk about statistics using the terminology and methods they learned as a graduate student. As most present graduate students might feel a bit squeamish about "teaching an old dog new tricks," particularly if the student has to do the teaching and the major professor doing the learning, it is well to have a common language between student and professor.

Second, and perhaps more important, there is after all some value in learning "traditional" statistics. Having said that, it should be pointed out that much of the present text is directed toward looking at some "traditional" statistical methods in some very non-traditional ways. This, of course, brings out the other half of the bargain. If the author can expect certain things of the reader, then surely, the reader can fairly wish to know "What's the payoff?"

1.2 Raison d-etre' of this Text

Perhaps one of the simplest truisms in graduate schools is that students in general fear having to take statistics. After the "requirement" is finally satisfied, some students will have lost their fear and begin to understand the rationale for statistics; unfortunately, it would appear that statistics teachers have rarely approached having 100% of their students come to that understanding. Some students will continue in their fears, and yet another group will have had their fears replaced by hours of manipulative drudgery.

In the end, a goodly number of students are able to execute a rather intricate process, such as the analysis of covariance, by spending a sufficient length of time at a calculator. Whether very many of the students of traditional presentations are able to understand the relationship between the many manipulations is doubtful.

Thus, the specific aim of this text is to present several useful statistical methods in such a way that the calculations are minimized, and that an understanding of the statistical method employed can be more readily attempted.

1.3 Different Meanings of "Regression"

One thing that should be fairly clear to most readers is that any given word may mean different things to different people. Put more succinctly, a person's phenomenological world is likely to show some differences regarding the semantics used. In particular, different statisticians would mean different things by the statement, "A regression approach was used." To oversimplify, more typical approaches to statistics will usually include a discussion and methodology for simple (one-predictor) regression, and a discussion and examples for multiple regression (more than one predictor). One such text is Roscoe (1969). A newer development is the use of linear models to effect solutions to statistical problems, including the analysis of variance problem. Mendenhall (1968) covered both the linear model approach and some of the more usual regression problems. Ward and Jennings (1973) presented an extensive use of their particular approach to problem solving by regression. They emphasize the statement of a problem in natural language terms and then translate that language to a computer solution. Both Mendenhall and Ward and Jennings emphasize to some degree the understanding and use of matrices. Kelly, Beggs and McNeil (1969) use an approach similar to Ward and Jennings, and use a particular computer program (which is included in their text) for solutions to their approach. Yet another approach to regression methodology was given by Draper and Smith (1966); they consider many different kinds of regression problems in a manner which might be said to "catalog", or cover, most regression situations.

Within the context of the previously described approaches to regression, the present text is to some degree eclectic, and to some degree, individually unique in it's approach. Borrowing of ideas are noted from Ward and Jennings, Kelly, Beggs and McNeil, Bottenberg and Ward (1963) and Schmid (1967). That is, a linear model approach will be consistently used throughout. On the other hand, the particular models used would seem a bit unusual to the donors.

Some mention should be made in regard to the computer. It is necessary that the reader have access to some computer. This should be easily satisfied as most colleges and universities either have at least one computer of their own or have some type of hook-up with a computer at some other location. In either case, most computer facilities will already have several statistical programs working, including a regression program. As an example, computers manufactured by International Business Machines (IBM) have an accompanying statistical package that includes a general purpose multiple regression program.

Because a computer is necessary, a natural question is "How much computer programming is necessary?" The answer is, very little. As a multiple regression program will usually already be working (in computer language, they will have a "canned" program for multiple linear regression), only a few cards are necessary to make the program work (These cards will vary from facility to facility). Most colleges and universities employ academic programmers who help faculty and students in using the existing ("canned") programs.

Because a computer will effect the solution ("do the dirty work"), some readers might be curious as to how a regression solution is effected by the computer. While these details are not necessary to study the present text, it might be pointed out that solutions to multiple regression problems are effected through the use of matrices. Those interested in viewing the matrix solution to the regression problems using linear models are directed to Mendenhall (1968) or Ward and Jennings (1973).

1.4 Topics Considered

The text is organized so that the earlier chapters allow the reader to travel on familiar ground. Chapter Two reviews simple correlation and regression. Chapter Three, which contains the groundwork for the remainder of the text, introduces the use of multiple regression and multiple correlation in relation to a computer solution. Chapter Four reconsiders the familiar t test in a regression formulation; Chapter Five uses a regression formulation for the one-way analysis of variance situation. Chapter Six considers some selected multiple comparison procedures using regression; Chapter Seven presents the treatments X subjects design (repeated measures design); and Chapter Eight presents a formulation of the two-way analysis of variance by regression. Chapter Nine presents a method that is rarely considered in the first or second course in applied statistics, a two-way analysis of variance with disproportionate cell frequencies. More advanced texts, such as Winer (1971) give a much more complex solution, using a hand calculator. That the disproportionate case is not considered earlier in the typical approach is unfortunate, since much data concerning human beings will normally be disproportionate.

Chapter Ten considers two practical regression solutions, stepwise and setwise regression. The focus is upon the backward (that is, with a full regression down to a single variable or set of variables) solutions, though reference is made to other types of solutions.

Chapter Eleven considers the solution to the technique called the analysis of covariance. The analysis of covariance can be used if the experimenter has chosen a "control" variable prior to an experiment such that the control variable will reduce the variation in such a way that the experimenter can run a more efficient experiment. Typical control variables are intelligence test data or pre-tests on the test used as the final criterion. The use of regression brings the technique within the conceptual understanding of the covariation process, rather than the solution to endless equations. Multiple covariates can be easily incorporated in the regression approach; those readers who have previously solved a covariance problem without the aid of a computer will be most appreciative of the relative simplicity afforded by the regression solution.

Chapter Twelve, on part and partial correlation, is directed more to the understanding of these concepts rather than effecting an efficient computer program for their solution. Efficient computer programs for these two techniques are of course available and are described in Chapter Twelve.

Related to part correlation is a technique known as residual gain analysis; the residuals from regressing the post-test scores on the pre-test scores are used as the criterion, and analysis of variance is performed on the residuals. The study of trends is the focus of Chapter Thirteen. In addition to polynomial trends, the use of trend analysis in a repeated measures design is explored.

The final chapter, Chapter Fourteen, provides a short summary and attempts to place in perspective the focus of the present text in relation to data analysis in general, and other texts relating to regression and other approaches to statistics.

CHAPTER TWO

CORRELATION AND REGRESSION: A BRIEF REVIEW

2.1 Correlation

The present chapter has three purposes; 1) to very briefly review a few topics in regression and correlation; 2) to set that review in the terminology that follows in the remainder of the text; and 3) to lead into the use of the computer.

Correlation is a measure of the relationship between two variables, and a correlation coefficient (r) can vary between -1 and 1. The correlation between two variables, X and Y, is given by

$$r = \frac{\Sigma XY - \frac{(\Sigma X)(\Sigma Y)}{n}}{\sqrt{\left(\Sigma X^2 - \frac{(\Sigma X)^2}{n}\right)\left(\Sigma Y^2 - \frac{(\Sigma Y)^2}{n}\right)}}, \qquad (2.1)$$

where

r = a symbol for the correlation coefficient,
ΣX = the sum of the X scores,
ΣY = the sum of the Y scores,

ΣX^2 = the sum of the squares of each X score,

ΣY^2 = the sum of the squares for each Y score,
ΣXY = the sum of the product of the corresponding X and Y scores.

To review the use of equation 2.1, scores from two administrations of the Kuhlman Anderson Intelligence test scores can be correlated. In the data that follows (Table 2.1), Paluck (1968) was interested in finding the long term "reliability" of the Kuhlman-Anderson test. The test was administered three times in the school with which he was associated: Form A was given in the first grade, Form D was given in the fourth grade, and Form G was given in the seventh grade.

To illustrate the calculations involved, Form A is correlated with Form G.

TABLE 2.1

TEST SCORES FROM TWO ADMINISTRATIONS OF THE KUHLMAN-ANDERSON INTELLIGENCE TEST

Student	Form "A" (X)	Form "D"	Form "G" (Y)
1	116	103	110
2	117	110	104
3	119	106	107
4	115	96	93
5	100	98	95
6	120	120	127
7	116	113	114
8	102	107	99
9	109	104	113
10	111	93	105
11	125	106	118
12	112	99	97
13	108	115	113
14	120	114	123
15	110	106	104
16	115	98	102
17	115	126	118
18	113	100	107
19	112	105	114
20	110	129	100
21	114	102	104
22	111	94	101
23	104	82	93
24	116	103	106
25	101	103	103

Table 2.2 shows the necessary calculations to find r.

TABLE 2.2

CALCULATION OF CORRELATION BETWEEN FORM A (X) AND FORM G (Y) OF THE KUHLMAN-ANDERSON INTELLIGENCE TEST

Student	X	X^2	Y	Y^2	XY
1	116	13456	110	12100	12760
2	117	13689	104	10816	12168
3	119	14161	107	11449	12733
4	115	13225	93	8649	10695
5	100	10000	95	9025	9500
6	120	14400	127	16129	15240
7	116	13456	114	12996	13224
8	102	10404	99	9801	10098
9	109	11881	113	12769	12317
10	111	12321	105	11025	11655
11	125	15625	118	13924	14750
12	112	12544	97	9409	10864
13	108	11664	113	12769	12204
14	120	14400	123	14129	14760
15	110	12100	104	10816	11440
16	115	13225	102	10404	11730
17	115	13225	118	13924	13570
18	113	12769	107	11449	12091
19	112	12544	114	12996	12768
20	110	12100	100	10000	11000
21	114	12996	104	10816	11856
22	111	12321	101	10201	11211
23	104	10816	93	8649	9672
24	116	13456	106	11236	12296
25	101	10201	103	10609	10403
Σ	2811	316979	2670	287090	301005

From Table 2.2, $\Sigma X = 2811$, $\Sigma X^2 = 316979$, $\Sigma Y = 2670$, $\Sigma Y^2 = 287090$, $\Sigma XY = 301005$.

Thus,

$$r = \frac{301005 - \frac{(2811)(2670)}{25}}{\sqrt{\left(316979 - \frac{(2811)^2}{25}\right)\left(287090 - \frac{(2670)^2}{25}\right)}},$$

$$r = \frac{301005 - 300214.8}{\sqrt{(316979 - 316068.8)\ (287090 - 285156)}},$$

$$r = \frac{790.2}{1326.8},$$

$r = .5955$ or $r = .60$.

2.2 The Variance Interpretation of Correlation

If the correlation coefficient is squared, the resulting figure (r^2) is an indication of how much of the variance of one variable is accountable from the variance of the other variable. For the data on the Kuhlman-Anderson Intelligence Test, r = 60; thus $r^2 = .36$. Therefore we can say that 36 percent of the variance of either variable is accountable from the other variable. The remaining 64 percent of the variance is unexplained (or error) variance.

if r squared ⇒ r^2 indicates the % of the variance of either variable accountable from the other variable.

2.3 Variability and Correlation

The size of a correlation coefficient is affected by considerations other than the relationship of the two tests. Considering the data on the Kuhlman-Anderson Intelligence Test reported herein, the Form A tests ranged from 100 to 125. If a larger range was used (say from 80 to 125) a higher value would have been found for r. Several factors might enter here. The original data may have included individuals with lower scores, but they may have been systematically eliminated (held back a grade, transferred to another school in the same area, placed in special education classes, etc.). Thus it is not always wise to talk about a correlation coefficient without reporting other information concerning the group on which the correlation coefficient was found.

2.4 Prediction

A natural question comes to mind with information such as is recorded in this chapter regarding intelligence test scores. While correlation helps answer the question, "How closely are the two scores related?" an equally intriguing question is, "Given the first grade intelligence scores, can we predict the seventh grade intelligence scores?" Computationally, the solution to the latter question is very similar to the correlation computations. The more important concern is that the reader understand what is meant by prediction.

First, prediction involves an antecedent variable, i.e., one variable occurs before the other variable. The first variable, which can be more simply called the predictor variable, is measured (through tests or whatever is considered important under the circumstances). A reference group is used, which may well be the present group of students in a class. The second variable is measured. This variable is called the criterion variable. A prediction equation can then be formulated. The process of prediction is accomplished through the methodology of regression.

2.5 Regression

If the end result of measurement for purposes of prediction is the formation of a prediction equation, such an equation is given by

$$\hat{Y} = b_0 + b_1 X \quad , \qquad (2.2)$$

where

$\hat{Y}$ = the predicted value (this can be read Y hat),

b_0 = a number which would be the predicted value for Y when X = 0,

b_1 = the regression coefficient, and

X = the predictor variable.

It should be emphasized that the first measured variable, the predictor variable, is labeled X. Likewise, the second variable, the criterion variable, is labeled Y. With this in mind, the values for b_0 and b_1 still remain unknown at this point. The equation for b_1 is

$$b_1 = \frac{\Sigma XY - \frac{(\Sigma X)(\Sigma Y)}{n}}{\Sigma X^2 - \frac{(\Sigma X)^2}{n}} \quad . \qquad (2.3)$$

If there were interest in finding a prediction equation for the Kuhlman-Anderson Intelligence Test scores in the seventh grade from those test scores in the first grade, essentially the same information needed for correlation will be needed for regression. Also, the similarity between the two equations should be noted. For the Kuhlman-Anderson Intelligence Test scores,

$$b_1 = \frac{301005 - \frac{(2811)(2670)}{25}}{316979 - \frac{(2811)^2}{25}} \quad ,$$

$$b_1 = \frac{301005 - 300214.8}{316979 - 316068.8} \quad ,$$

$$b_1 = \frac{790.2}{910.2} \quad ,$$

$$b_1 = .87.$$

Now, b_0 can be easily found:

$$b_0 = \overline{Y} - b\overline{X} \quad . \qquad (2.4)$$

For the present (Intelligence Test scores) data,

$$\overline{X} = \frac{2811}{25} = 112.44 \text{ and } \overline{Y} = \frac{2670}{25} = 106.8\text{; thus,}$$

$b_0 = 106.8 - (.87)(112.44)$,

$b_0 = 106.8 - 97.8$,

$b_0 = 9$.

Thus, by substituting in the values for b_0 and b_1, the prediction equation is $\hat{Y} = 9 + .87X$. For this data, other than as an additive constant, the value of b_0 has little meaning. An $X = 0$ would mean an Intelligence Test score of zero, which is largely meaningless. Actually, predictions should only be made within the range of the original X scores, in this case, 100-125.

To find a predicted value for any individual can be accomplished using equation 2.4. For student 1, the score on Form A is 116; thus, X = 116, and

$\hat{Y} = 9 + (.87)(116)$,

$\hat{Y} = 9 + 100.92$,

$\hat{Y} = 109.92$.

That $\hat{Y}$ is not equal to Y (the real score) is not surprising. There will be some error in prediction for at least some values if $r < 1$. The difference, $Y - \hat{Y} = 110 - 109.92 = .08$ is the amount of error involved in prediction with the first student. It would be advantageous for the reader to try other values of X to see how well the prediction equation works. It would also be worthwhile to find correlations between Form A and Form D, and between Form D and Form G.

An equation closely related to equation 2.2 is given by

$$Y = b_0 + b_1X_1 + e \qquad (2.5)$$

where

Y = the actual score,

e = the error in prediction, and

b_0, b_1 and X_1 have the same meaning as in equation 2.2.

Both equations 2.2 and 2.5 are referred to as regression equations. In equation 2.2, the focus was on predicting the Y values; equation 2.5 is concerned not only with predicting the Y values, but with including a measurement of the error in prediction also. The computations for finding b_0 and b_1 are identical for the two equations.

2.6 The Standard Error of Estimate

The standard error of estimate is a measure of dispersion for regression, and can be thought of as a standard deviation for the regression situation. While the usual standard deviation measures dispersion from the mean, the standard error of estimate measures dispersion from a regression line. The equation for the standard error of estimate can be given as

$$s_{y.x} = \sqrt{\frac{(Y - \hat{Y})^2}{n - 2}} \, , \qquad (2.6)$$

where $Y - \hat{Y}$ is the difference between the actual criterion score and the estimate of the criterion score from the regression equation.

When a hand calculator is used, a more common equation for the standard error of estimate is given by

$$s_{y.x} = s_y \sqrt{(1 - r^2) \; \frac{n - 1}{n - 2}} \, , \qquad (2.7)$$

where s_y is the standard deviation of the Y scores and r is the correlation between X and Y. For the data in Table 2.1, the standard error for the prediction of the Form G scores from the Form A scores is

$$s_{y.x} = 8.98 \sqrt{(1 - (.60)^2) \; \frac{(24)}{23}} = 7.33.$$

(8.98 is the standard deviation of the Form G scores).

2.7 Using the Computer

The preceding presentation on regression and correlation has been made for review purposes rather than purporting to be anything new. The important change is that these calculations can be routinely performed and reported by the use of a regression program through the use of a computer. As most readers are familiar with the hand calculation methods, the same kind of problem can be reconceptualized and solved through the use of the computer. In the exercises that conclude this chapter, it would be worthwhile to attempt to solve the problems first by doing them either by hand or by using a calculator, and then set them up for a computer solution.

The following chapter considers in more detail the process of using the computer with a regression problem, and also considers the concept of multiple correlation.

2.8 Summary

Two closely related concepts, correlation and regression (prediction) are reviewed. The equation for correlation is

$$r = \frac{\Sigma XY - \frac{(\Sigma X)(\Sigma Y)}{n}}{\sqrt{\left(\Sigma X^2 - \frac{(\Sigma X)^2}{n}\right)\left(\Sigma Y^2 - \frac{(\Sigma Y)^2}{n}\right)}} \quad . \qquad (2.1)$$

The regression coefficient can be found by

$$b_1 = \frac{\Sigma XY - \frac{(\Sigma X)(\Sigma Y)}{n}}{\Sigma X^2 - \frac{(\Sigma X)^2}{n}} \quad . \qquad (2.3)$$

After b_1 has been found, the constant, b_0, is found by

$$b_0 = \overline{Y} - b\overline{X}. \qquad (2.4)$$

Using the values for b_0 and b_1 found from the preceding equations, the prediction equation is

$$\hat{Y} = b_0 + b_1 X. \qquad (2.2)$$

A form of the regression equation that includes the actual scores rather than the predicted scores is given by

$$Y = b_0 + b_1 X_1 + e \qquad (2.5).$$

The standard error of estimate is given by

$$s_{y.x} = s_y \sqrt{(1 - r^2)\frac{n - 1}{n - 2}} \quad . \qquad (2.7)$$

and can be thought of as a standard deviation for prediction.

While these equations represent the more common (and tedious) "hand" methods of calculation, computer programs typically available at most computer facilities can routinely perform the necessary calculations.

EXERCISES

2.1a) Find the correlation between Form A and Form D for Paluck's data in Table 2.1.

b) Find the correlation between Form D and Form G for Paluck's data in Table 2.1.

2.2a) Find the prediction equation for predicting Form D scores from Form A scores for Paluck's data.

b) Find the prediction equation for predicting Form G scores from Form D scores for Paluck's data.

2.3a) Find the standard error of estimate for 2 (a).

b) Find the standard error of estimate for 2 (b).

CHAPTER THREE

MULTIPLE REGRESSION AND MULTIPLE CORRELATION

3.1 Introduction

The present chapter introduces the situation when several different scores are available for each member in a group. If the interest in the multiple measurements is to predict some criterion, then the situation is called multiple regression. If the purpose is to find the relationship between a group of variables and a single variable, then the situation is called multiple correlation. The researcher may also wish to use both concepts with the same data.

One very important point should be made. The remaining chapters in this text assume that the reader has access to a computer facility. This assumption seems reasonable in the light that most colleges and universities have a computer available to them. With this computer capability it would be a needless waste of time to do hand calculations on such things as multiple regression, multiple correlation, and the many related concepts. Using the computer does not necessitate a great deal of computer programming sophistication. Learning the important details in running a program such as the multiple regression program should not exceed two hours. While many other programs will be referred to in the next several chapters, they simply represent offshoots of the general multiple regression programs which are widely available.

3.2 Multiple Regression

The process of multiple regression can be thought of as using several predictors to predict a single criterion variable. The process is similar in concept to using one predictor (as in Chapter Two). Additional predictors can be included. As a simple example of multiple regression, suppose both Form A and Form D are simultaneously used to predict the intelligence scores on Form G for the data presented in Table 2.1. A prediction equation can be formed by the equation

$$Y = b_0 + b_1X_1 + b_2X_2 + e, \qquad (3.1)$$

where

Y = the intelligence score on Form G for each individual,
X_1 = the intelligence score on Form A for each individual,
X_2 = the intelligence score on Form D for each individual,
b_0 = the constant term,

b_1 = the regression coefficient for X_1,

b_2 = the regression coefficient for X_2, and

e = the error in prediction with this set of data.

Equation 3.1 is very similar to equation 2.5, with the exception of another variable (scores of Form D) being added. The use of more than one predictor will usually allow for less error in prediction than would occur using only a single variable. Thus, equation 3.1 would use two previous measures of intelligence (Forms A and D administered in the first and fourth grade, respectively) to predict intelligence scores in the seventh grade (Form G). In general, the b_0 and b_1 values will be different for equations 2.5 and 3.1. In a manner similar to equation 3.1, the researcher can include as many variables as are deemed feasible. In general, the multiple regression situation can be written as

$$Y = b_0 + b_1X_1 + b_2X_2 + . . . + b_nX_n + e. \qquad (3.2)$$

Equations 3.1 and 3.2 are sometimes referred to as <u>linear models</u>. Essentially, a linear model is an equation that expresses a criterion value as the weighted sum of several predictor variables. The weighting is done by the regression coefficients.

3.3 An Example of Multiple Linear Regression

The following hypothetical data can be useful to illustrate the concept of multiple linear regression. Suppose the interest is to predict success in typing from the knowledge of intelligence and manual dexterity. The researcher collects information available on each subject prior to their typing experience of one semester. The following information is available after the completion of the experiment. See Table 3.1.

TABLE 3.1

TYPING SPEED, INTELLIGENCE SCORES AND MANUAL DEXTERITY SCORES
(HYPOTHETICAL DATA)

Typing Speed Y	Intelligence Score X_1	Manual Dexterity Score X_2
35	120	38
27	98	28
32	102	32
29	106	22
27	94	30
38	123	43
25	96	31
36	108	46
35	115	40
31	128	35
27	90	27
35	110	31
19	94	25
17	95	24
32	116	33

First, a linear model can be made to represent the data in Table 3.1:

$$Y = b_0 + b_1X_1 + b_2X_2 + e.$$

The preceding equation is of the same form as equation 3.1, and briefly says that the Y variable (Typing Speed) is to be predicted from the X_1 variable (Intelligence Score) and the X_2 variable (Manual Dexterity Score). The b_0, b_1, b_2 and e values are values that will be found in the least squares process. The data from Table 3.1 was analyzed by the multiple regression process by using a multiple purpose computer program. Similar programs are likely to be found in almost every university computer facility. A typical printout is found in Table 3.2.

For a person viewing the results of a printout for the first time, a first look at Table 3.2 can be forbidding. Actually, a considerable amount of useful information can be extracted. First of all, the prediction equation can be taken directly from the printout. The Y variable is labelled variable number 1, X_1 is labelled variable number 2 and X_2 is labelled variable number 3. If the regression coefficients are read directly from the printout, the linear model is

$$Y = -6.34753 + .19451\ X_1 + .47418\ X_2 + e. \qquad (3.3)$$

The error in prediction with each score is given in the Table of Residuals, the latter part of Table 3.2.

Some of the more salient features of Table 3.2 are worthy of some discussion. The heading MEAN refers to the mean of the three variables taken separately. The STANDARD DEVIATION is likewise the standard deviations for each separate variable. The CORRELATION X VS Y is the correlation of each predictor variable with the criterion. The REGRESSION COEFFICIENT is of course the regression coefficients for each variable in this particular model. The STD. ERROR OF REG. COEF. is the standard error of each regression coefficient. COMPUTED T VALUE is a t test for each regression coefficient in this particular model. BETA refers to the beta coefficient. A beta coefficient is a regression coefficient for each variable if the scores had first been changed to standard scores (z scores). The reader is referred to DuBois (1957) for a discussion and usage of beta coefficients. DEPENDENT refers to the dependent, or criterion variable (typing speed). INTERCEPT is of course the b_0 value in equation 3.3. The STANDARD ERROR OF ESTIMATE is in regard to the Y variable using the two predictors, and is analogous to the standard error of estimate encountered in Chapter Two. The remaining portions of Table 3.2 are more easily approached with some background in multiple correlation, the subject of the next section.

3.4 Multiple Correlation

The multiple correlation coefficient is a correlation between a single criterion and several predictors. Conceptually, if the several predictors are used to arrive at a predicted score for each value of Y using equation 3.3 then the multiple correlation is the correlation between the Y scores and the predicted Y scores ($\hat{Y}$). There are several different computational forms for the multiple correlation coefficient (see, for example, Tatsuoka, 1971); however, pragmatically, the multiple correlation coefficient is routinely printed out from running the program for multiple linear regression.

Referring back to Table 3.2, the multiple correlation coefficient (R) is given as .83961. As an exercise, the student can run a simple correlation between the Y VALUES and the Y ESTIMATE VALUES from the TABLE OF RESIDUALS to confirm this multiple correlation coefficient (See exercise 3.1). The square of the multiple correlation coefficient, R^2, is given as .70495 and is to $(.83961)^2$; $1 - R^2$ is equal to .29505 and is given on the printout. If the ANALYSIS OF VARIANCE FOR THE REGRESSION is inspected, some interesting relationships can be found. If the sum of squares attributable to regression (370.33130) is divided by the total sum of squares (525.33301), the result is identically equal to R^2. If the deviation from regression sum of squares

TABLE 3.2

Multiple Regression Printout

VARIABLE NO.	MEAN	STANDARD DEVIATION,	CORRELATION X VS Y	REGRESSION COEFFICIENT	STD. ERROR OF REG.COEF.	COMPUTED T VALUE	BETA
2	106.33333	11.99206	0.73089	0.19451	0.10498	1.85276	0.38078
3	32.33333	6.99659	0.78775	0.47418	0.17994	2.63526	0.54160
DEPENDENT							
1	29.66666	6.12566					

INTERCEPT -6.34753

MULTIPLE CORRELATION 0.83961

STD. ERROR OF ESTIMATE 3.59400

MULTIPLE CORRELATION SQUARED 0.70495

ONE MINUS MULTIPLE CORRELATION SQD 0.29505

ANALYSIS OF VARIANCE FOR THE REGRESSION

SOURCE OF VARIATION	DEGREES OF FREEDOM	SUM OF SQUARES	MEAN SQUARES	F VALUE
ATTRIBUTABLE TO REGRESSION	2	370.33130	185.16565	14.33525
DEVIATION FROM REGRESSION	12	155.00171	12.91681	
TOTAL	14	525.33301		

TABLE OF RESIDUALS

CASE NO.	Y VALUE	Y ESTIMATE	RESIDUAL
1	35.00000	35.01190	-0.01190
2	27.00000	25.99100	1.00900
3	32.00000	28.66573	3.33427
4	29.00000	24.70197	4.29803
5	27.00000	26.16133	0.83867
6	38.00000	37.96632	0.03368
7	25.00000	27.02452	-2.02452
8	36.00000	36.47128	-0.47128
9	35.00000	34.98775	0.01225
10	31.00000	35.14542	-4.14542
11	27.00000	23.96077	3.03923
12	35.00000	29.74759	5.25241
13	19.00000	23.79044	-4.79044
14	17.00000	23.51076	-6.51076
15	32.00000	31.86299	0.13701

(155.00171) is divided by the total sum of squares, the result is identically equal to $1 - R^2$. The value R^2 is often referred to as the percent of error variance (or non-accountable variance). The multiple correlation coefficient can thus be thought of as the square root of the percent of the accountable variance.

It should be mentioned that the multiple correlation coefficient will always be between 0 and 1; it will likewise be at least as large and, as most likely larger than, any of the separate correlations of the predictor variables with the criterion. The test of significance for the multiple correlation coefficients can be directly made. The F value given on the printout, 14.33525, can be compared to the tabled value from the F table with 2 and 12 degrees of freedom. In that 14.33525 is greater than the value at the .01 level, the multiple correlation coefficient is significantly different from 0 ($p < .01$).

3.5 A Note on Decimals

The only reason that five place accuracy has been maintained in the previous section is that the particular computer system used had five decimal accuracy. In reporting the results in a published form, typically no more than three decimal points would be included.

3.6 Summary

Two related techniques, multiple regression and multiple correlation, are introduced in this chapter. Multiple regression occurs when more than one predictor is used to predict a criterion. Multiple correlation, on the other hand, is the correlation between one variable and a group of variables. The use of a computer is indespensible in any research application using either of these concepts. In that the two concepts are quite closely related, they will normally be available from a single printout from the computer.

EXERCISES

3.1 Find the correlation between the Y values and the Y estimate values from Table 3.2.

3.2 Find the multiple regression equation for predicting the Form G intelligence test scores from the knowledge of the Form A and Form D scores given in Table 2.1 (That is, using Form A and Form D as predictors, and with Form G as the criterion, form the prediction equation).

CHAPTER FOUR

THE t TEST IN A REGRESSION APPROACH

4.1 Introduction

The t test is a familiar statistical technique that allows two groups to be compared on the same criterion. So that the regression approach can be fairly contrasted, it is worthwhile to present an application of the t test in its usual format.

4.2 An Application of the t Test

The students in a school are randomly placed in one of two different sections to learn ninth grade English. Group One is using programmed materials which cover the same material as is covered in Group Two, except that group two is taught in a more conventional manner. After six weeks, the two classes are given the same test.

X_1	X_2
25	25
24	23
23	21
23	17
22	22
21	20
18	15
17	14
16	12
16	10
16	10
15	12
14	11
13	10
13	7
13	6
12	6
11	8
10	4
9	7

Here, $\Sigma X_1 = 331$, $\Sigma X_1^2 = 5939$, $\overline{X} = 16.55$;

$\Sigma X_2 = 260$, $\Sigma X_2^2 = 4148$, $\overline{X} = 13.00$.

The usual method to evaluate such a situation is given in equation 4.1:

$$t = \frac{\bar{X}_1 - \bar{X}_2}{\sqrt{\left(\frac{\Sigma X_1^2 - \frac{(\Sigma X_1)^2}{n_1} + \Sigma X_2^2 - \frac{(\Sigma X_2)^2}{n_2}}{(n_1 + n_2 - 2)}\right)\left(\frac{1}{n_1} + \frac{1}{n_2}\right)}}, \quad (4.1)$$

For this specific example,

$$t = \frac{16.55 - 13.00}{\sqrt{\left(\frac{5939 - \frac{(331)^2}{20} + 4148 - \frac{(260)^2}{20}}{(20 + 20 - 2)}\right)\left(\frac{1}{20} + \frac{1}{20}\right)}},$$

$$t = \frac{3.55}{\sqrt{\frac{1228.95}{38}\left(\frac{1}{10}\right)}},$$

$$t = \frac{3.55}{\sqrt{3.23}},$$

$$t = \frac{3.55}{1.80} = 1.97.$$

This t value fails to reach significance at the .05 level on a two-tailed test since, for 38 degrees of freedom, a t value of 2.03 or higher (approximately) would be required.

4.3 A Regression Approach to the t Test

What initially might seem a very novel use of regression will allow a solution to the two-group independent t-test situation. Briefly, the scores serve as the criterion, and the group membership (either Group One, programmed materials, or Group Two, conventional approach) can be used as the predictor variables. To accomplish this process, two "dummy" or binary coded variables can be formed. A "dummy" or binary variable is one that is recorded as a "1" if the characteristic is present or "0" if the characteristic is absent. For the two group situation, a student will be in either Group One or Group Two; if he is in Group One, then the binary variable for Group One students would be represented with a 1. For Group Two students, their "value" (or "score") on the Group One variable is 0. Likewise, Group Two students can have a binary variable such that a 1 is recorded if the student is from Group Two, and a 0 if they are not. To complete the t test for the data in Table 4.1, two binary predictors, X_1 and X_2, can be formed for using a regression approach:

X_1 = 1 if the score is from a member of Group One; 0 otherwise,

X_2 = 1 if the score is from a member of Group Two; 0 otherwise,

A linear model can be written for this situation:

$$Y = b_0 + b_1X_1 + b_2X_2 + e_1, \qquad (4.2)$$

where

Y = the criterion score,

b_0 = the Y-intercept,

b_1 = the regression coefficient for X_1,

b_2 = the regression coefficient for X_2,

e_1 = the error involved in prediction.

The preceding information can be put in a table (see Table 4.2) which is particularly helpful for preparation of the data cards for submission to the computer. One card can be prepared for each of the observed scores, together with the information regarding group membership.

The conceptualizing that usually takes place during the use of the t-test might center around the question, do the means differ significantly? On the other hand, in a regression formulation, the researcher's thought process may involve using the knowledge of group membership to predict the criterion scores. In the final analysis, both approaches use the same linear model.

If the multiple regression program is used with the data from Table 4.2, with the two predictor variables, X_1 and X_2, and with the Y variable as the criterion, the probable result is that the program will not run and will simply report back something like "MATRIX SINGULAR SELECTION IS SKIPPED AS REQUESTED." For the person unfamiliar with the computer, many different reactions can occur, from disgust to "I knew it couldn't do it." Without going into technical details, the problem is one of supplying too much information. Going back to one of the predictor variables, say X_1, either a 1 or a 0 is recorded for every criterion measure. The next column, X_2, is simply the reverse of X_1, that is, if there was a 0 in X_1, then X_2 has to be a 1. Thus, only one of the predictor variables is necessary to impart all the information regarding group membership.

For the information in Table 4.2, X_1 was used as the predictor of the criterion variable, using a general purpose multiple regression program. Portions of the regression solution are in Table 4.3.

The intercept (b_0) is also included. This value is 13.00 and is the mean of Group Two, the group that was coded as 0 on the X_1 variable. The multiple correlation, R, is .304097. Since there is only one predictor variable, this value is a Pearson product-moment correlation of the test scores with group membership. Because the group membership variable is binary, the correlation reported is actually a point-biserial correlation coefficient. Both the standard error of estimate and an analysis of variance for the regression are included in the printout. An option is available in the multiple regression program for a table of residuals if they are desired. Table 4.3 contains the printout (not including the table of residuals) for the data in Table 4.2. The regression coefficient is for the predictor variable X_1; we have, in effect, set $b_2 = 0$ by this approach. If 3.55 (the regression coefficient) is added to 13.00 (the intercept), the mean of Group One can be found and is 16.55.

It can be noted that the results that were obtained by the usual t-test were also found by using the regression approach. In addition to the computed t value (t = 1.97403), the F value of 3.897 is also equal to t^2. Additionally, if the correlation coefficient is squared ($r^2 = .0925$), this indicates that 9.25 percent of the criterion variance can be accounted for by knowledge of group membership.

4.4 The Hypothesis Tested in the Regression Formulation

While the results of the two different approaches to the t test situation can be seen to give identical results, the reasons for this outcome are not intuitively obvious. To help illuminate the situation, a look at the hypothesis tested in a regression formulation would seem helpful.

Whereas the typical null hypothesis for the two-group situation is usually stated as $\mu_1 = \mu_2$ (the mean of Group One equals the mean of Group Two), a similar statement can be made for the regression case; returning to equation 4.2,

$$(Y = b_0 + b_1X_1 + b_2X_2 + e_1)$$

the null hypothesis can be stated as $b_1 = b_2 = b$; that is, the regression coefficient is the same for the group membership variables. The statement, $b_1 = b_2 = b$ is called a <u>restriction</u>.

TABLE 4.2

REGRESSION FORMULATION OF THE t-TEST

Y	X_1	X_2
25	1	0
24	1	0
23	1	0
23	1	0
22	1	0
21	1	0
18	1	0
17	1	0
16	1	0
16	1	0
16	1	0
15	1	0
14	1	0
13	1	0
13	1	0
13	1	0
12	1	0
11	1	0
10	1	0
9	1	0
25	0	1
23	0	1
21	0	1
17	0	1
22	0	1
20	0	1
15	0	1
14	0	1
12	0	1
10	0	1
10	0	1
12	0	1
11	0	1
10	0	1
7	0	1
6	0	1
6	0	1
8	0	1
4	0	1
7	0	1

TABLE 4.3

MULTIPLE REGRESSION SOLUTION FOR t-TEST SITUATION

SELECTION 1

Variable No.	Mean	S.D.	Correlation X vs Y	Regression Coefficient	Standard Error of Regression Coefficient	Computed t Value	Beta
1	0.50000	0.50637	0.30497	3.55000	1.79835	1.97403	0.30497
Dependent							
3	14.77500	5.89431					
Intercept		13.00000					
Multiple Correlation		0.30497					
Standard Error of Estimate		5.68689					

ANALYSIS OF VARIANCE FOR THE REGRESSION

Source of Variation	Degrees of Freedom	Sum of Squares	Mean Squares	F Value
Attributable to regression	1	126.02502	126.02502	3.89678
Deviation from regression	38	1228.94995		
Total	39	1354.97485		

If that restriction is entered in equation 4.2, then

$$Y = b_0 + bX_1 + bX_2 + e_2,$$

$$Y = b_0 + b(X_1 + X_2) + e_2. \qquad (4.3)$$

But $X_1 + X_2$ will always be 1; thus

$$Y = b_0 + b + e_2. \qquad (4.4)$$

Several comments are necessary regarding equations 4.3 and 4.4. First, the error term has been changed from e_1 to e_2 in that placing restrictions on the data will almost always result in a different amount of error in prediction (usually the amount of error, in squared units, will increase). In equation 4.4, b_0 and b are simply constants and can in fact be combined into a single constant, c. (That is, $c = b_0 + b$). Then equation 4.4 becomes

$$Y = c + e_2. \qquad (4.5)$$

What equation 4.5 says, essentially, is the Y values are being predicted by a constant term. Put more simply, equation 4.5 is attempting to predict all scores as being the mean of the two groups. Thus, all knowledge of group membership has been excluded. Without going into considerably more detail at this point, it is safe to say that the use of equation 4.5 would result in a correlation of 0, and the calculations presented in the printout in Table 4.2 are sufficient for the successful execution of the t test.

4.5 Assumptions Regarding the Use of the t Test

To use the t test, three assumptions are involved:
(1) The scores should come from two independent random samples,
(2) The two groups are equally variable,
(3) The scores in both groups are normally distributed.

Much research has been expended on the validity of the t test when one or more of the assumptions are violated. If the first assumption is not fulfilled, the test is, for practical purposes, meaningless. However, this requirement is within the control of the experimenter, and if proper precautions are observed it can be considered satisfied (In the vernacular, the first assumption has been called the "don't cheat" assumption. If the researcher collects his data in a fair manner, this assumption is usually satisfied).

Several empirical studies (among them Boneau (1960) and Dayton (1967)) have been conducted concerning the latter two assumptions. The conclusions tend to indicate that if the

violation of the assumptions are not too serious (admittedly a value judgment), the t test can be considered as valid. If the researcher is unwilling to accept some departure from the two requirements (normal distribution and equal variance), then he can consider using one of the so-called non-parametric tests (See Siegel, 1956).

4.6 Other Varieties of t Tests

Two additional types of t tests that have not been considered in this chapter are the related t test and the one-sample t test (See Williams, Harlow and Houston, 1969). There are two reasons for their present omission. The first reason is pragmatic; these particular t tests are as readily done with more traditional techniques as they are with regression techniques. A second reason, in relation to the related t test, is that it's presentation is delayed until Chapter Six, where the related t test is considered in a more general context with the treatments X subjects (or repeated measures) design.

4.7 Summary

The t test can be reconceptualized into a regression format, using the group membership as the predictor variables with the test scores serving as criterion. Because the t-test will involve only two groups, a single group membership variable is sufficient to accomplish the regression solution. One of the two groups can be coded as 1, and the second group can be coded as 0. Using the binary (1 or 0) variable as predictor, a regression equation can be formed. Typical regression computer printouts usually include a considerable amount of information beyond reporting a t test. Also included are the intercept (mean of the zero-coded group), the regression coefficient (if added to the mean of the zero-coded group, the mean of the group coded "1" results), the point-biserial correlation between the group membership variables and the test scores variable, the standard error of measurement, the standard error of the regression coefficient, the beta value and an analysis of variance for the regression.

EXERCISES

4.1 Using the regression approach, test for differences between the means of Group 1 and Group 2:

Group 1	Group 2
8	26
13	17
12	15
13	22
19	25
7	15

4.2 To test the comparative amount of implementation of a workshop on self-enhancing education, two groups of teachers were formed. The first group of teachers had attended a week long workshop in self enhancing education and during the course of the school year had several in-service activities relating to implementing the self enhancing process (Randolph and Howe, 1966) in their classrooms. At the end of the school year, trained observers used interaction analysis adapted to the self enhancing education concept to measure the several categories of classroom interaction. Simultaneously, a control group of teachers from the same school district and teaching at the same grade levels was also observed. Data from the category Gathers and Accepts Thoughts of Students, taken from Williams (1973) follow:

Number of Occurrences for the Category

Gathers and Accepts Thoughts of Students

Self Enhancing Education Teachers	Control Teachers
69	31
0	0
0	0
0	0
0	0
0	0
0	0
0	0
6	0
41	0
111	0
2	8
4	0
15	68
0	59
0	1
15	0
0	0
16	1
106	4
31	0
20	0
91	0
	0
	0
	0

Find the t value through the use of regression.

CHAPTER FIVE

ANALYSIS OF VARIANCE BY REGRESSION

5.1 The Analysis of Variance

Typically, the analysis of variance is approached in a somewhat different manner from the t test, and a rather different, and somewhat cumbersome process is given. Using a regression approach, the close relationship between the analysis of variance and the t test should become obvious.

The analysis of variance is a technique that allows a comparison of the means from several groups simultaneously. The technique is widely described in introductory texts in applied statistics. The focus here is on the conceptualization of the method rather than the many calculations.

An application of the analysis of variance taken from Williams, Harlow and Houston (1969) follows:

An investigator was interested in viewing the effects on memorization of four different approaches with educable retarded children. Consider a situation where twelve mentally retarded pupils are randomly selected from a junior high special education program, with the investigator then placing three children in each of four treatment groups. Since past learning would vary from child to child and could consequently contaminate the results of the research a neutral task requiring little past learning would be utilized--the learning of pairs of unrelated nouns (for example, corn--bus). All subjects, instructed to associate the nouns, would be told that they would be evaluated after the session as to their ability to recall the second noun upon hearing the first. With twenty pairs of nouns presented at the rate of one every eight seconds, the groups would differ in their approach to the learning of the task. Subjects in Group One would read the pair of nouns from a programming device revealing the words for the full eight seconds. Group Two would receive the pair of nouns by having them orally repeated by the investigator during the eight seconds. Group Three would be presented the nouns through pictorial representations via a programming device. The noun pairs would be presented orally by the investigator to Group Four and the subjects would then repeat the pairs aloud. All subjects would be tested immediately after the learning session. The data for this hypothetical study are recorded in Table 5.1.

TABLE 5.1

EDUCABLE RETARDED SUBJECTS ON A PAIRED-ASSOCIATE LEARNING TASK

	Group One	Group Two	Group Three	Group Four
	X_1	X_2	X_3	X_4
	4	13	11	10
	2	10	9	9
	0	7	7	8
Σ	6	30	27	27
$\bar{X}$	2	10	9	9

In their presentation, Williams, Harlow and Houston give all the necessary equations to perform the analysis of variance; they are not repeated here. The outcome of using the analysis of variance is a summary table for the analysis of variance. The summary table for the data in Table 5.1 is given in Table 5.2.

TABLE 5.2

SUMMARY TABLE FOR THE ANALYSIS OF VARIANCE FOR THE PAIRED-ASSOCIATE LEARNING TASK

Source of Variation	df	Sum of Squares	Mean Squares	F
Among groups	3	123.00	41.00	9.11
Within groups	8	36.00	4.50	
Total	11	159.00		

5.2 A Regression Approach to the Analysis of Variance

A regression solution can be generated to complete the analysis of the data in Table 5.1.

To conceptualize the problem for a regression analysis, it is helpful to define a set of binary predictors. Four binary predictors can be defined to correspond to the four groups:

X_1 = 1 if the score is from a member of Group One; 0 otherwise,

X_2 = 1 if the score is from a member of Group Two; 0 otherwise,

X_3 = 1 if the score is from a member of Group Three; 0 otherwise,

X_4 = 1 if the score is from a member of Group Four; 0 otherwise.

A linear model can be written for this situation:

$$Y = b_0 + b_1X_1 + b_2X_2 + b_3X_3 + b_4X_4 + e_1, \quad (5.1)$$

where

Y = the criterion score,

b_0 = the Y-intercept,

b_1 = the regression coefficient for X_1,

b_2 = the regression coefficient for X_2,

b_3 = the regression coefficient for X_3,

b_4 = the regression coefficient for X_4, and

e_1 = the error involved in prediction.

The information regarding group membership and the criterion scores can be put into a format similar to the formulation of the t test in Chapter Four and is found in Table 5.3.

TABLE 5.3

REGRESSION FORMULATION FOR ONE-WAY ANALYSIS OF VARIANCE

Y	X_1	X_2	X_3	X_4
4	1	0	0	0
2	1	0	0	0
0	1	0	0	0
13	0	1	0	0
10	0	1	0	0
7	0	1	0	0
11	0	0	1	0
9	0	0	1	0
7	0	0	1	0
10	0	0	0	1
9	0	0	0	1
8	0	0	0	1

Again, it can be remembered that the last column is actually not adding any new information and can be considered redundant. If b_4 is set equal to 0, the prediction equation can be rewritten as

$$Y = b_0 + b_1X_1 + b_2X_2 + b_3X_3 + e_1. \quad (5.2)$$

Using this setup, the previous data was analyzed with a general purpose multiple regression program.

Again, the printout will normally include the means, standard deviations, correlations with the criterion, regression coefficients, standard errors of the regression coefficients, computed t values, and the beta coefficients. The intercept for this data is given as 9.00 (the mean of Group Four, the "omitted" group in equation 5.2). The multiple correlation, R, is equal to .87954, and the standard error of estimate is 2.1213. In the analysis of variance for regression, the following summary table (Table 5.4) is routinely printed out (there is also included in the printout the previously mentioned items, but they are omitted here).

TABLE 5.4

ANALYSIS OF VARIANCE FOR REGRESSION

Source of Variation	df	Sum of Squares	Mean Squares	F
Attributable to Regression	3	123.00	41.00	9.11
Deviation from Regression	8	36.00	4.50	
Total	11	159.00		

The usage of the regression program should become apparent. Not only is the data available that normally is a part of analysis of variance, but also, a measure of the amount of variance that can be accounted for by the predictor variables can be found. Here R = .87954 and, therefore, R^2 = .7755; thus 77.55 percent of the criterion variance can be accounted by knowledge of the group membership.

One additional advantage is pedagogical. As the student becomes familiar with the regression approach, he can more fully understand the logic of both regression and experimental analysis.

5.3 Hypothesis in the Regression Solution

In a manner similar to section 4.4, the null hypothesis for the analysis of variance, $\mu_1 = \mu_2 = \mu_3 = \mu_4 = \mu$, can be tested in terms of the regression coefficients: $b_1 = b_2 = b_3 = b_4 = b$; that is, the regression coefficients are the same for each group membership variable. If this restriction is substituted into equation 5.1, then

$$Y = b_0 + bX_1 + bX_2 + bX_3 + bX_4 + e_2,$$

$$Y = b_0 + b(X_1 + X_2 + X_3 + X_4) + e_2. \qquad (5.2)$$

But $X_1 + X_2 + X_3 + X_4$ will always be equal to 1 (since a person will be a member of exactly one of four groups); thus

$$Y = b_0 + b + e_2. \qquad (5.3)$$

Again, e_2 is the new error term under the restriction $b_1 = b_2 = b_3 = b_4 = b$. Also, b_0 and b are constants and can be combined into a single constant, c, in a manner similar to section 4.4. Equation 5.3 becomes

$$Y = c + e_2, \qquad (5.4)$$

a form identical to equation 4.5. Again, the mean of the four groups is used to predict each score, with knowledge of group membership excluded. Again, the use of equation 5.4 as a regression equation would result in a correlation of 0. Thus, the summary table given in Table 5.4 is sufficient for the analysis of variance.

5.4 Assumptions Involved in the Analysis of Variance

The assumptions underlying the F test for a one-way analysis of variance are quite similar to those of the t test, the differences reflecting that more than two groups can be involved:

1) The scores come from independent random samples of the same parent population.
2) All groups are equally variable.
3) The scores of each group are normally distributed.

Much of the considerations concerning the F test for a one-way analysis of variance are similar to those of the t test. Norton (1952) investigated card populations with various degrees of violations of the second and third assumption. Norton found that the form of the distributions did not seriously affect the probability levels. The heterogeneity of variance was seen to be a somewhat more important consideration. When the two assumptions were both violated, then the probability level became somewhat questionable. In general, Norton's findings would allow the researcher to use the analysis of variance procedure with moderate violations of the last two assumptions. Lindquist (1953) has discussed in considerable detail the study completed by Norton.

5.5 Summary

The analysis of variance has been reconceptualized from a regression viewpoint, using the group membership as the predictor variable with the test scores serving as criterion. The actual process of achieving the analysis of variance is very similar to the process for achieving the t test given in Chapter Four. In the t test situation, there are two groups; using one of the group membership variables is sufficient to accomplish the analysis. In the analysis of variance with k groups, k - 1 of the group membership variables (it does not matter which group membership variable is omitted) are sufficient to accomplish the analysis. Thus, the t test situation is exactly analogous to the analysis of variance situation in a regression formulation, taking into account the number of groups in the analysis.

EXERCISES

5.1 Given the following data:

Group One	Group Two	Group Three	Group Four
9	7	13	14
9	6	11	12
8	4	10	9
7	4	7	7
5	2	7	6
4	1	6	4

Complete the analysis of variance and construct a summary table.

5.2 Given the following data:

Group One	Group Two	Group Three
9	14	18
8	11	16
7	6	17
6	5	13
4		9
3		
1		

Complete the analysis of variance and construct a summary table.

5.3 Given the following data:

Group One	Group Two	Group Three	Group Four	Group Five
19	20	13	12	22
18	19	12	8	20
15	16	10		19
13	16	10		19
8	14	10		15
5	14			
	13			

Complete the analysis of variance and construct a summary table.

CHAPTER SIX

MULTIPLE COMPARISONS IN A REGRESSION APPROACH

6.1 Multiple Comparisons

The rejection of the null hypothesis $\mu_1 = \mu_2 = \mu_3 = \ldots = \mu$ would rarely seem to be completely satisfying. It is only natural to ask, if there are differences, where are those differences? Since the overall F test does not provide the solution, then it would seem natural to seek a direct solution to the researcher's problem(s). If multiple use of the t test were made, the reported probability level would be seriously violated; hence the use of multiple t tests would be inappropriate. What is appropriate depends upon the situation. Several multiple comparison tests have been devised to satisfy a particular demand or analysis upon the data. Thus, it would seem that there is no best multiple comparison method that universally fits all situations; rather, if the researcher can point out his comparisons of interest, he can proceed to choose an appropriate multiple comparison method. Rather than attempting to "catalog" the many multiple comparison methods, two useful tests are described using the regression approach. These two tests are Dunnett's test for comparing several treatments with a control group and Tukey's test. Other tests can of course be put in a regression format, as has been pointed out by Williams (1972b).

6.2 The Concept of Error Rate

Three different kinds of error rate that apply to the multiple comparisons situation have been discussed in detail by Ryan (1959, 1960). These are:

$$\text{Per comparison} = \frac{\text{No. of comparisons incorrectly called significant}}{\text{total number of comparisons}}; \quad (6.1)$$

$$\text{Per experiment} = \frac{\text{No. of comparisons incorrectly called significant}}{\text{total number of experiments}}; \quad (6.2)$$

and

$$\text{Experimentwise} = \frac{\text{No. of experiments containing erroneous statements of significance}}{\text{total number of experiments}}. \quad (6.3)$$

It can be seen that in general the three error rates will be different, with the error rate per comparison being the least stringent, and the error rate per experiment being the most stringent. Ryan (1959, 1962) has indicated that the use of the per comparison error rate should be discouraged, and one of the other approaches adopted. The two tests to be described here both retain an experimentwise error rate.

6.3 A Priori and A Posteriori Tests

Another consideration in regard to multiple comparison tests is the concept of a priori and a posteriori tests. An a priori test is one in which the comparisons have been decided on in advance of the gathering of data. On the other hand, a posteriori tests allow the researcher to decide on the hypotheses to be tested even after he has inspected the data. Thus, the a posteriori tests allow the researcher the flexibility to consider relationships of interest after he has completed his preliminary data analysis. The cost of this flexibility is loss in power; that is, the tests where the researcher has set his hypotheses to be tested in advance of the data collection will generally have somewhat more power and will allow the null hypothesis to be rejected more often than if the hypotheses have not been set in advance.

A very crude, but useful rule to follow in choosing between an a priori test and an a posteriori test is the following: if you know what you're doing, use an a priori test; otherwise, use an a posteriori test. In other words, the a priori tests are quite useful in theory testing and theory building situations; the a posteriori tests are more of a general purpose type of test.

6.4 Dunnett's Test for Comparisons of Several Treatment Groups with a Control

Dunnett (1955, 1964) devised a test that would allow the comparisons of several treatment groups with a control group and still retain an experimentwise error rate. This test could also be used whenever an experimenter wished to test a group which he might call the "experimental group" against several existing (but different) groups.

For example, a business educator may have devised a new approach to teaching beginning typewriting. He may find that instead of finding one typical approach to teaching typewriting there may be several methods being used. Rather than lumping all of the existing methods together and calling them a control group, it would seem more logical to test the new approach against each existing group separately, but in a single experiment. Dunnett's test is appropriate for this situation. Dunnett's test, from the regression approach of the present text, is a direct byproduct of having run the analysis of variance by regression. As an example, exercise 5.1 can be used. The data are repeated in Table 6.1.

TABLE 6.1

DATA FOR DUNNETT'S TEST

Control Group Group One	Group Two	Group Three	Group Four
9	8	13	15
8	7	10	12
6	8	12	10
3	6	11	17
4	6	14	11

$\overline{X}_1 = 6.0$, $\overline{X}_2 = 7.0$, $\overline{X}_3 = 12.0$, $\overline{X}_4 = 13.0$

Suppose the interest is in comparing the Control Group to Groups One, Two and Three.

Viewing the problem from a regression viewpoint, it is helpful to define four binary predictors:

X_1 = 1 if the score is from a member of the control group (Group One); and 0 otherwise,

X_2 = 1 if the score is from a member of Group Two; and 0 otherwise,

X_3 = 1 if the score is from a member of Group Three; and 0 otherwise,

X_4 = 1 if the score is from a member of Group Four; and 0 otherwise.

A linear model can be written for this situation:

$$Y = b_0 + b_2 X_2 + b_3 X_3 + b_4 X_4 + e_1, \qquad (6.4)$$

where

b_0 = the Y-intercept,

b_2 = the regression coefficient for Group Two,

b_3 = the regression coefficient for Group Three,

b_4 = the regression coefficient for Group Four, and

e_1 = the error involved in prediction.

It can be noticed that the control group has seemingly been left out. However, if equation 6.4 is solved for the expected value for a member of the control group,

$$E(Y) = b_0 + b_2(0) + b_3(0) + b_4(0),$$

$E(Y) = b_0$. The expectancy for a member of the control group is by definition $\overline{X}_1$. Thus, a least squares solution for b_0 is $\overline{X}_1$, the mean of the control group.

For a member in Group Two, the expected value is

$$E(Y) = b_0 + b_2(1) + b_3(0) + b_4(0),$$
$$E(Y) = b_0 + b_2,$$
$$E(Y) = \overline{X}_0 + b_2. \qquad (6.5)$$

A least squares solution for the expectancy of a given number of Group Two is the mean of Group Two;

Thus $\overline{X}_2 = \overline{X}_1 + b_2$ from equation 6.5, or

$$\overline{X}_2 - \overline{X}_1 = b_2. \qquad (6.6)$$

Likewise

$$b_3 = \overline{X}_3 - \overline{X}_1 \text{ and } b_4 = \overline{X}_4 - \overline{X}_1.$$

Equation 6.4 can be rewritten

$$Y = \overline{X}_1 + (\overline{X}_2 - \overline{X}_1)X_2 + (\overline{X}_3 - \overline{X}_1)X_3 + (\overline{X}_4 - \overline{X}_1)X_4 + e_1. \qquad (6.7)$$

Equation 6.7 lists precisely the comparisons of interest for comparing several treatments with a control. Since equation 6.4 (and, therefore, equation 6.7) is the same model as was given for a one-way analysis of variance, this approach also yields results identical to the analysis of variance situation. Thus, using equation 6.4, it can be seen that these two useful results can be obtained simultaneously: the usual analysis of variance as one part of the output, and Dunnett's test as the other part.

The information necessary for a regression solution, with equation 6.4 as the linear model, can be conveniently placed in tabular form (see Table 6.2).

TABLE 6.2

REGRESSION FORMULATION FOR COMPARING SEVERAL TREATMENTS WITH A CONTROL

Y	X_0	X_1	X_2	X_3
9	1	0	0	0
8	1	0	0	0
6	1	0	0	0
3	1	0	0	0
4	1	0	0	0
8	0	1	0	0
7	0	1	0	0
8	0	1	0	0
6	0	1	0	0
6	0	1	0	0
13	0	0	1	0
10	0	0	1	0
12	0	0	1	0
11	0	0	1	0
14	0	0	1	0
15	0	0	0	1
12	0	0	0	1
10	0	0	0	1
17	0	0	0	1
11	0	0	0	1

TABLE 6.3

OUTPUT OF MULTIPLE REGRESSION PROGRAM

Variable No.	Mean	Standard Deviation	Correlation X vs Y	Regression Coefficient	Std. Error of Reg. Coef.	Computed t Value	Beta
3	0.25000	0.44426	-0.40109	1.00001	1.36014	0.73522	0.12033
4	0.25000	0.44426	0.40109	6.00001	1.36014	4.41130	0.72197
5	0.25000	0.44426	0.56153	7.00001	1.36014	5.14652	0.84230
Dependent 1	9.50000	3.69210					
Intercept		5.99999					
Multiple Correlation		0.84515					
Std. Error of Estimate		2.15058					

ANALYSIS OF VARIANCE FOR THE REGRESSION

Source of Variation	Degrees of Freedom	Sum of Squares	Mean Squares	F Value
Attributable to Regression	3	185.00027	61.66675	13.33340
Deviation from Regression	16	73.99973	4.62498	
Total	19	259.00000		

For the data in Table 6.2, the general purpose multiple regression program was used. Table 6.3 contains the printout from that analysis. The variable number in Table 6.3 refers to the order in Table 6.2; the criterion variable is variable number 1; variable 2 refers to the control group, variable 3 to Group Two, variable 4 to Group Three and variable 5 to Group Four. Because variable 2 refers to the Control Group, no information appears in the printout using that variable number. The table of residuals has not been included herein.

Table 6.3 contains the previously mentioned items. It can be recalled that $\bar{X}_1 = 6.0$, $\bar{X}_2 = 7.0$, $\bar{X}_3 = 12.0$, $\bar{X}_4 = 13.0$. The intercept is 6.0 (within rounding error) and is $\bar{X}_1$. Also, $b_2 = 1 = \bar{X}_2 - \bar{X}_1$, and is in keeping with equation 6.7. Similar statements could be made concerning b_3 and b_4. The computed t values in Table 6.3 are identically the same values as would result from the use of Dunnett's test. It is only necessary to compare each of these values to Dunnett's table for the test of significance. From Table V, a computed t value of 3.51 is needed for significance at the .01 level on a two-tailed test. Thus, both Groups Two and Three are significantly higher than the Control Group.

6.5 Tukey's Test

A useful test which can be used on an a posteriori basis and retain an experimentwise error rate is Tukey's* (1953) test. Quite often, Tukey's test is used when a significant F value has been found, and the interest is in pinpointing where the differences are. It is not necessary that the overall F test be applied to use Tukey's test, however. Also, Tukey's test is usually applied to all pairs $\binom{n}{2}$ of means in the situation where there are more than two groups. Thus, if there were four groups, then there would be $\binom{4}{2}$ or 6 comparisons.

For the data presented in Table 6.1, there are $\binom{4}{2}$, or 6 comparisons of interest (that is, all possible comparisons of pairs) for Tukey's test.

They are the following:

*Tukey has devised several tests involving multiple comparisons. The test described here has often been called the honesty significant different (H.S.D.) test.

$\bar{X}_1$ to $\bar{X}_2$,
$\bar{X}_1$ to $\bar{X}_3$,
$\bar{X}_1$ to $\bar{X}_4$,
$\bar{X}_2$ to $\bar{X}_3$,
$\bar{X}_2$ to $\bar{X}_4$, and
$\bar{X}_3$ to $\bar{X}_4$.

Now, there are several ways that Tukey's test can be achieved, even using a regression approach. The particular method described here has one major advantage over other descriptions of the calculations of Tukey's test: it is by far the easiest to accomplish, using a computer. A much more elegant solution is given by Williams (1972b).

6.6 A Simplified Solution to Tukey's Test

Tukey's test can be accomplished with k - 1 successive uses of regression equations (where k is the number of groups) where models similar to equation 6.4 are solved; in each successive solution, a different group is omitted from the equation.

Thus, for the data in Table 6.1, the solution given for Dunnett's test also includes three of the six comparisons of interest for Tukey's test. Each of the succeeding models also include three of the six comparisons of interest, but the second model duplicates an already calculated comparison.

To be more specific, Group Two can be omitted from the model, yielding

$$Y = b_0 + b_1X_1 + b_3X_3 + b_4X_4 + e_1. \qquad (6.5)$$

The calculated t values for these comparisons are

t = -.735 for comparing $\bar{X}_1$ to $\bar{X}_2$ (this was also available from the first model, equation 6.4)

t = 3.676 for comparing $\bar{X}_3$ to $\bar{X}_2$, and

t = 4.411 for comparing $\bar{X}_4$ to $\bar{X}_2$.

Then, Group Three can be omitted from the model, yielding

$$Y = b_0 + b_1X_1 + b_2X_2 + b_4X_4 + e_1 . \qquad (6.6)$$

The calculated t values for these comparisons are

$t = -4.411$ for comparing $\overline{X}_1$ to $\overline{X}_2$ (this was also available from the first model, equation 6.4)

$t = -3.676$ for comparing $\overline{X}_2$ to $\overline{X}_3$ (this was also available from the second model, equation 6.5)

$t = .735$ for comparing $\overline{X}_4$ to $\overline{X}_3$.

A change in sign from one equation to the next in computed t values is to be expected. In the first model, whose results are shown in Table 6.3, the computed t value for comparing $\overline{X}_1$ to $\overline{X}_2$ is .735. From equation 6.5, the computed t value for comparing $\overline{X}_2$ to $\overline{X}_1$ is -.735. This is because the means are being compared in a different order. The first test showed $\overline{X}_2 > \overline{X}_1$. As we would surely expect, the second test showed $\overline{X}_1 < \overline{X}_2$.

To evaluate these t values, the Tables of the Studentized Range Statistic are to be used, but a modification is first necessary. Using the Table III, the value of q for 4 groups and $df_w = 16$, at the .01 level is $q = 5.192$. To evaluate the computed t values, the value for q should be divided by $\sqrt{2}$: the critical value $= \frac{q}{\sqrt{2}} = \frac{5.192}{1.414} = 3.672$.

Table 6.4 contains the results for Tukey's test.

TABLE 6.4

TUKEY'S TEST IN A REGRESSION FORMULATION

Comparison	t
$\overline{X}_1$ to $\overline{X}_2$	.735
$\overline{X}_1$ to $\overline{X}_3$	4.411*
$\overline{X}_1$ to $\overline{X}_4$	5.147*
$\overline{X}_2$ to $\overline{X}_3$	3.676*
$\overline{X}_2$ to $\overline{X}_4$	4.411*
$\overline{X}_3$ to $\overline{X}_4$	.735

*Significant at the .01 level

Four of the six comparisons are significant at the .01 level.

6.7 Other Multiple Comparison Methods

The two methods given here are but two of the commonly used tests. Other tests include Duncan's (1955) Multiple Range test, which is similar to Tukey's test, but does not retain an experimentwise error rate; the Neuman (1939) Keuls (1952) test, also similar to Tukey's test, but focusing upon the order of the means; Dunn's (1961) test, which is particularly useful on an *a priori* basis when a very small number of comparisons are of interest; orthogonal comparisons, a method particularly useful in testing for trend; and Scheffe's (1953) test, which can be used to test *any* hypothesis concerning the means while retaining an experimentwise error rate. Most of these tests can be accomplished through the approach given here.

6.8 Summary

Two multiple comparison methods, Dunnett's test for comparing several treatments with a control, and Tukey's test, which allows the comparison of every combination of means, are given in a regression approach. The particular approaches given here are simple applications of models that also yield the usual analysis of variance.

EXERCISES

6.1 Use Dunnett's test to compare Group One (as the control group) to Group Two, Three and Four in Table 5.1.

6.2 Use Tukey's test for the data in Table 5.1.

6.3 Complete Dunnett's test for the data in exercise 5.2, with Group One serving as the control group.

6.4 Use Tukey's test for the data in exercise 5.2. NOTE: Because there are an unequal number of scores in each group, both Dunnett's test and Tukey's test are only approximate.

6.5 Complete Dunnett's test for the data in exercise 5.3, with Group Two serving as the control group.

6.6 Use Tukey's test for the data in exercise 5.3.

CHAPTER SEVEN

THE TREATMENTS X SUBJECTS DESIGN

7.1 Introduction

The treatments X subjects design is a design in which the treatments are all administered in succession to each subject, rather than working with different groups of subjects as would be the case in the simple randomized design (the usual one-way analysis of variance). The treatments X subjects design allows an increase of the precision of an experiment in that each subject serves as his own control. One limitation of this design is that if learning occurs from treatment to treatment, this method would be inapplicable. Stated another way, there should be no carry-over effect from one treatment to the next treatment. If, on the other hand, the effects of the experiment are only temporary, this design could be successfully employed. The treatments X subjects design is discussed in detail in Lindquist (1953).

7.2 An Example of the Treatments X Subjects Design

Suppose a researcher is interested in investigating the differences in sense modalities in paired-associate learning of educable mentally retarded children. Three approaches to paired associate learning are to be investigated: learning through the auditory sense, through the visual sense and through a simultaneous exposure to both senses. Ten subjects are available, and 30 paired associate items are presented under each of the three treatment conditions to each subject on three successive days; the particular treatment used with a given subject is administered in a random order, with the order or presentation randomized separately for each subject. The results of this hypothetical experiment are reported in Table 7.1.

TABLE 7.1

THREE TREATMENT METHODS OF PAIRED-ASSOCIATE LEARNING WITH EDUCABLE MENTALLY RETARDED SUBJECTS

Subject	Treatment One	Treatment Two	Treatment Three
1	18	27	15
2	17	24	14
3	14	13	12
4	5	8	6
5	11	14	10
6	9	12	8
7	14	16	15
8	12	17	9
9	22	21	16
10	10	18	15

7.3 A Regression Approach to the Treatments X Subjects Design

Viewing the problem from a regression approach, a solution can be obtained in stages. First, a Full Model is constructed. Very simply, a full model will contain all of the information available for a given situation. For the treatments X subjects design, two bits of information are available for each criterion score, the treatment involved, and the subject involved. If a set of thirteen binary predictors are constructed, the full model is

$$Y = b_0 + b_1X_1 + b_2X_2 + b_3X_3 + b_4X_4 + b_5X_5 + b_6X_6 + b_7X_7 + b_8X_8 + b_9X_9 + b_{10}X_{10} + b_{11}X_{11} + b_{12}X_{12} + b_{13}X_{13} + e_1, \quad (7.1)$$

where

Y = the criterion score,

X_1 = 1 if the score is from subject number 1; 0 otherwise,

X_2 through X_{10} are defined similar to X_1,

X_{11} = 1 if the score is from a member of Treatment One; 0 otherwise,

X_{12} = 1 if the score is from a member of Treatment Two; 0 otherwise,

X_{13} = 1 if the score is from a member of Treatment Three; 0 otherwise,

e_1 = the error in prediction.

The regression coefficients are defined in terms of the corresponding predictor, with b_0 being the Y-intercept. The information from the preceding can be conveniently put into a table (see Table 7.2) so that it can be readily put on punch cards.

As happened before, we actually have too much information. That is, X_{10} is determined by the previous nine predictors. Thus, it can simply be omitted as a predictor. This is the same as letting $b_{10} = 0$. Likewise, X_{13} is dependent upon X_{11} and X_{12}, and can be omitted as a predictor. This also is the same as setting $b_{13} = 0$. The full model will then use eleven predictors and be referred to as selection one. It will also be called Model I.

Two restricted models can be defined. First, ten binary predictors can be constructed, one for each subject. The last predictor can be omitted. The regression equation becomes:

$$Y = b_0 + b_1X_1 + b_2X_2 + b_3X_3 + b_4X_4 + b_5X_5 + b_6X_6 + b_7X_7 + b_8X_8 + b_9X_9 + e_2, \qquad (7.2)$$

where

Y = the criterion variable,

X_1 through X_9 are defined the same as in the full model (Model I),

b_0 = the Y-intercept,

b_1 = the regression coefficient corresponding to X_1,

b_2 through b_9 are similarly defined,

e_2 = the error in prediction for subjects,

$b_0 - b_9$ will, in general, have different values in equations 7.1 and 7.2.

This information can be called Model 2 and yields the subjects effect.

Finally, a model (Model 3) can be defined for treatments (columns) and is

$$Y = b_0 + b_{11}X_{11} + b_{12}X_{12} + e_3, \qquad (7.3)$$

where

Y = the criterion score,

X_{11} and X_{12} are defined as before,

b_0 = the Y-intercept,

b_{11} = the regression coefficient for X_{11},

b_{12} = the regression coefficient for X_{12},

e_3 = the error in prediction for treatments.

The variable X_{13} was deleted here for the same reason that it was deleted in the full model; that is, it introduces no new information, and is thus redundant. Model 3 will be called selection three.

The regression formulation for the treatments X subjects design is given in Table 7.2.

TABLE 7.2

REGRESSION FORMULATION FOR TREATMENTS X SUBJECTS DESIGN

Y	X_1	X_2	X_3	X_4	X_5	X_6	X_7	X_8	X_9	X_{10}	X_{11}	X_{12}	X_{13}
18	1	0	0	0	0	0	0	0	0	0	1	0	0
27	1	0	0	0	0	0	0	0	0	0	0	1	0
15	1	0	0	0	0	0	0	0	0	0	0	0	1
17	0	1	0	0	0	0	0	0	0	0	1	0	0
24	0	1	0	0	0	0	0	0	0	0	0	1	0
14	0	1	0	0	0	0	0	0	0	0	0	0	1
14	0	0	1	0	0	0	0	0	0	0	1	0	0
13	0	0	1	0	0	0	0	0	0	0	0	1	0
12	0	0	1	0	0	0	0	0	0	0	0	0	1
5	0	0	0	1	0	0	0	0	0	0	1	0	0
8	0	0	0	1	0	0	0	0	0	0	0	1	0
6	0	0	0	1	0	0	0	0	0	0	0	0	1
11	0	0	0	0	1	0	0	0	0	0	1	0	0
14	0	0	0	0	1	0	0	0	0	0	0	1	0
10	0	0	0	0	1	0	0	0	0	0	0	0	1
9	0	0	0	0	0	1	0	0	0	0	1	0	0
12	0	0	0	0	0	1	0	0	0	0	0	1	0
8	0	0	0	0	0	1	0	0	0	0	0	0	1
14	0	0	0	0	0	0	1	0	0	0	1	0	0
16	0	0	0	0	0	0	1	0	0	0	0	1	0
15	0	0	0	0	0	0	1	0	0	0	0	0	1
12	0	0	0	0	0	0	0	1	0	0	1	0	0
17	0	0	0	0	0	0	0	1	0	0	0	1	0
9	0	0	0	0	0	0	0	1	0	0	0	0	1
22	0	0	0	0	0	0	0	0	1	0	1	0	0
21	0	0	0	0	0	0	0	0	1	0	0	1	0
16	0	0	0	0	0	0	0	0	1	0	0	0	1
10	0	0	0	0	0	0	0	0	0	1	1	0	0
18	0	0	0	0	0	0	0	0	0	1	0	1	0
15	0	0	0	0	0	0	0	0	0	1	0	0	1

Using three selections, each of the sources of variation can be separately determined. The treatments effect can be found as the portion "attributable to regression" for selection three; the subjects effect can be found as the portion "attributable to regression" from selection two; and the error portion can be found as the portion "deviation from regression" for selection one. Actually, any one of the selections could have been omitted and the other portion could have been found as a residual. Those results are found in Table 7.3.

TABLE 7.3

ANALYSIS OF VARIANCE FOR TREATMENTS X SUBJECTS DESIGN

Source of Variation	Degrees of Freedom	Sum of Squares	Mean Squares	F
Treatments	2	136.27	68.13	11.52
Subjects	9	521.20	57.91	
Error	18	106.39	5.91	
Total	29	763.86		

With 2 and 18 degrees of freedom, the F value given in Table 7.3 is significant at the .05 level.

Using the multiple correlations from each selection, the following additional results were found:

(a) With the full model, R = .92774, and R^2 = .8607.

(b) With the 9-predictor model system, that is, the "subject" effect, R = .82602, and R^2 = .6823.

(c) With the regression model for treatment effects, R = .42236, and R^2 = .1784.

Hence, it can be seen that the "subjects" accounted for the most variance.

While this entire analysis has been concerned with duplicating the treatments X subjects design described by Lindquist, exactly the same set of linear models could be written for the randomized block design as described by Edwards (1972).

7.4 Designs Similar to the Treatments X Subjects Design

There are other ways of conceptualizing experiments so that the analysis is identical to the one presented here for the treatments X subjects design. A simple example would occur when there is concern that a carry-over effect would contaminate the treatments in the experiment. In that case, the experimenter could "block" the experiment by choosing k blocks of subjects, where the members in each block are of comparable ability in regard to the criterion to be tested. Then, within each block, a subject is randomly assigned to each treatment group. This method is called randomized blocks. The analysis is identical to that presented here for the treatments X subjects design.

Another possibility is the random replications design. In general, this design is applicable when massive amounts of data are being analyzed. Conceptually, the design is used when groups (perhaps within a school or school system) are randomly assigned to a treatment. Thus, the school might appear as if it is running a complete, one-way design with each treatment method being employed on a different group of students. The experiment is then repeated in several more schools (or school systems). The mean of a group is used as the unit of analysis, rather than the individual student. While this may seem wasteful of data, on further examination, experiments of this type may have a greater impact on the education of students than would an experiment run in a single school (or school system). Also, the use of the mean of the group gives a useful measure of the success of the method with the typical student, particularly when the experiment is replicated in several different settings. This method is quite adequately treated by Lindquist (1953, Chapter 8).

A slightly different twist of the treatments X subjects design was employed by Grooters (1971). He was interested in doing a cost analysis of ten selected instructional departments at the four state colleges in North Dakota. His unit of analysis was the mean amount expended per student credit hour by department within a college. Only instructional costs were included; capital outlays were not considered. For example, if a department produced 4,000 student credit hours at a cost of \$60,000 (if, for example, five instructors were employed at an average salary of \$12,000), then the cost per student credit hour produced was $\frac{\$60{,}000}{4{,}000} = \$15.00$.
The data from the ten departments and the four colleges are found in Table 7.4.

TABLE 7.4

MEAN INSTRUCTIONAL COSTS BY DEPARTMENTS AT FOUR STATE COLLEGES FOR PRODUCING A STUDENT CREDIT HOUR (IN DOLLARS)

Department	College			
	Dickinson State College	Mayville State College	Minot State College	Valley City State College
Art	21.91	9.08	8.48	14.02
Biology	10.85	8.19	10.02	8.86
Business Education	8.40	7.59	7.61	7.51
Chemistry	10.32	15.52	15.49	18.21
Social Science	6.32	6.40	6.48	6.59
Mathematics	9.44	8.63	8.39	7.52
English	10.06	10.08	12.33	11.69
Music	19.93	18.43	34.48	17.53
Physical Education	9.51	14.22	12.84	11.85
Professional Education	8.01	10.26	14.43	11.03

The data in Table 7.4 could be analyzed by the same technique as the treatments X subjects design, with departments replacing subjects, and colleges replacing treatments.

7.5 Summary

The treatments X subjects design is a useful technique in that it allows the experimenter to use each subject as his own control. The treatments X subjects design can be used whenever the various treatments will not have any effect on the other treatments.

If there is danger that one treatment will effect one or more of the other treatments, then the treatments X subjects design cannot be used. However, if the subjects (or students) can be blocked on a relevant variable (such as intelligence) then one subject from each block can be randomly assigned to each treatment group. This kind of design is called a randomized blocks design. On a larger scale, whole classes may be included in an experiment similar to the randomized blocks design. In that case, replication of the experiment may take place in other schools (or school systems). This kind of design is called a random replications design. Both the randomized blocks design and the random replications design follow the same statistical analysis as the treatments X subjects design.

EXERCISES

7.1 Given the following data:

Subject	Treatment 1	Treatment 2	Treatment 3
1	2	5	9
2	6	12	27
3	10	14	33
4	9	13	30
5	8	9	27
6	6	11	24
7	2	4	12
8	4	12	24
9	0	3	3
10	3	7	11

Analyze the data and construct a summary table.

7.2 Analyze Grooter's data in Table 7.4. Both dimensions of the classification (colleges and departments) are likely to be of experimental interest; F values can then be reported for both sources of variation.

CHAPTER EIGHT

ANALYSIS OF VARIANCE WITH TWO-WAY CLASSIFICATIONS

8.1 Introduction

The concept of a two-way classification can be thought of as a simple extension of the one-way classification (one-way analysis of variance). For example, a researcher may be interested in differences between students in four colleges within a university (colleges of engineering, education, nursing, and arts and sciences) in regard to American College Test (ACT) scores. A second dimension of interest might be sex (male-female), so that a two-way classification scheme is used. Many other ways can be considered for two-way classifications depending upon the researcher's interest. Two variations of the two-way analysis of variance are considered:

1. both dimensions of classification are of research interest and is called a factoral design; and
2. one dimension represents levels for a control variable, a situation which is called treatments X levels.

8.2 Proportionality

An additional requirement of the two-way analysis of variance design is that the number of subjects in each cell are in the same proportion from row to row and from column to column. Because the concept of proportionality may be somewhat novel to some readers, a few comments seem appropriate. Empirically, the requirement is often satisfied by having an equal number of subjects in each cell (treatment combination). It is not necessary to have an equal number per cell to satisfy the proportionality requirement, however. The number of subjects in Table 8.1 would satisfy the proportionality requirement.

TABLE 8.1

PROPORTIONALITY FOR ROW TO ROW AND COLUMN TO COLUMN COMPAIRSONS

	Column 1	Column 2	Column 3	Column 4
Row 1	6	18	12	24
Row 2	9	27	18	36
Row 3	4	12	8	16

For rows, it can be noticed that row 1 has 2/3 the number of subjects that row 2 has for each corresponding cell. Row 1 has

3/2 the number of subjects that row 3 has for each corresponding cell. Also, row 2 has 9/4 the number of subjects that row 3 has for each corresponding cell. For columns, it can be noticed that column 1 has 1/3 the number of subjects as column 2 for each corresponding cell, 1/2 the number of subjects as column 3 for each corresponding cell, and 1/4 the number of subjects for each corresponding cell as column 4. Column 2 has 3/2 the number of subjects for each corresponding cell as column 3 and 3/4 the number of subjects for each corresponding cell as column 4. Thus, the proportionality requirement is satisfied. The reasons for the proportionality requirement are two: computational ease and orthogonality. In a day of computers, computational ease will seem less relevant. Orthogonality raises a different set of concerns, however. Orthogonality insures the independence of the row effect from the column effect, and vice versa. If disproportionality occurs, then there is some degree of mixing of row and column effects. For the present, only proportional situations will be considered. Recognizing the importance of naturally disproportional conditions in analyzing data regarding human beings, the disproportional case is given full treatment in Chapter Nine.

8.3 Factoral Designs

It is simpler to proceed by example. Suppose a researcher wishes to measure the effects of three different approaches to teaching arithmetic combined with four different methods of assigning homework. He has 24 students available to him, so he assigns the students randomly to one of the 12 (3 X 4) treatment combinations. When the experiment is concluded, he gives a standardized arithmetic test consisting of 20 items with the items in a multiple choice format. The three different methods of teaching arithmetic are 1) teaching arithmetic with the problems very similar to the final test; 2) teaching arithmetic with half the problems similar to the final test, and the other half dissimilar to the final test; and 3) teaching arithmetic with the problems dissimilar to the final test. The four different methods of homework are 1) problems in a multiple-choice format; 2) homework is of a project nature; 3) problems from the book in which the student supplies his own answer, and 4) no homework. The data for this experiment are in Table 8.2.

TABLE 8.2

DATA FOR METHOD OF TEACHING X TYPE OF HOMEWORK
(HYPOTHETICAL DATA)

Type of Homework	Method of Teaching: Very Similar Material to Final	Half Similar, Half Dissimilar Material to Final	Dissimilar Material to Final	Sum and Mean for Homework
Multiple	18	10	12	
Choice Items	10	6	10	
Project	5	2	9	
	3	2	3	
Student Supplies	7	6	4	
Own Answer	3	2	2	
No	2	7	10	
Homework	0	5	6	

8.4 A Regression Formulation for Two-Way Analysis of Variance

When proportionality is present, several alternative approaches will yield the same end products in the summary table. A simple to use approach is to successively analyze the data into three different one-way layouts. One layout would consider each treatment combination as a separate group. Thus, there would be (4)(3) = 12 groups. An analysis of variance, using the approach in Chapter Five could be generated by the following model (Model 1):

$$Y = b_0 + b_1X_1 + b_2X_2 + b_3X_3 + b_4X_4 + b_5X_5 + b_6X_6 + b_7X_7 + b_8X_8 + b_9X_9 + b_{10}X_{10} + b_{11}b_{11} + e_1, \qquad (8.1)$$

where

Y = the criterion variable,

b_0 = the Y-intercept (in this model, b_0 will equal the mean of Group Twelve),

X_1 = 1 if a score is from a member of Group 1; 0 otherwise,

$X_2 - X_{11}$ = 1 if a score is from a member of the group corresponding to the subscript number; 0 otherwise,

$b_1 - b_{11}$ = the regression coefficients for $X_1 - X_{11}$, and

e_1 = the error in prediction with this model.

A second model (Model 2) would include only information regarding the rows, disregarding the particular column:

$$Y = b_0 + b_{12}X_{12} + b_{13}X_{13} + b_{14}X_{14} + e_2, \qquad (8.2)$$

where

b_0 = the Y-intercept for this model (in this Model, b_0 will equal the mean of the fourth row, no homework),

X_{12} = 1 if the score is from a member in row 1 (Multiple Choice Items); 0 otherwise;

X_{13} = 1 if the score is from a member in row 2 (Project); 0 otherwise,

X_{14} = 1 if the score is from a member in row 3 (Student Supplies Own Answer); 0 otherwise,

$b_{12} - b_{14}$ = the regression coefficients corresponding to $X_{12} - X_{14}$, and

e_2 = the error in prediction for this model.

A third model (Model 3) would include only information regarding the columns, disregarding the particular row:

$$Y = b_0 + b_{15}X_{15} + b_{16}X_{16} + e_3, \qquad (8.3)$$

where

b_0 = the Y-intercept for this model (in this case, b_0 will equal the mean of the third column, dissimilar material to the final),

X_{15} = 1 if the score is from a member in column 1 (Very similar material to the final),

X_{16} = 1 if the score is from a member in column 2 (Half Similar, half dissimilar material to the final),

$b_{15} - b_{16}$ = are regression coefficients for $X_{15} - X_{16}$, and

e_3 = the error in prediction for this model.

A fourth model (Model 4), while not necessary when the data is proportional, is useful in understanding the process:

$$Y = b_0 + b_{12}X_{12} + b_{13}X_{13} + b_{14}X_{14} + b_{15}X_{15} + b_{16}X_{16} + e_4, \quad (8.4)$$

where

b_0 = the Y-intercept for this model (and is equal to the mean of Group Twelve, as was b_0 in Model 1),

$X_{12} - X_{16}$ = as defined in Models 2 and 3,

$b_{12} - b_{16}$ = are regression coefficients for $X_{12} - X_{16}$ for this model, and

e_4 = the error in prediction with this model.

All of the information regarding a regression solution is given in Table 8.3.

TABLE 8.3

REGRESSION FORMULATION OF THE TWO-WAY ANALYSIS OF VARIANCE

Y	X_1	X_2	X_3	X_4	X_5	X_6	X_7	X_8	X_9	X_{10}	X_{11}	X_{12}	X_{13}	X_{14}	X_{15}	X_{16}
13	1	0	0	0	0	0	0	0	0	0	0	1	0	0	1	0
5	1	0	0	0	0	0	0	0	0	0	0	1	0	0	1	0
6	0	1	0	0	0	0	0	0	0	0	0	1	0	0	0	1
2	0	1	0	0	0	0	0	0	0	0	0	1	0	0	0	1
6	0	0	1	0	0	0	0	0	0	0	0	1	0	0	0	0
4	0	0	1	0	0	0	0	0	0	0	0	1	0	0	0	0
7	0	0	0	1	0	0	0	0	0	0	0	0	1	0	1	0
5	0	0	0	1	0	0	0	0	0	0	0	0	1	0	1	0
5	0	0	0	0	1	0	0	0	0	0	0	0	1	0	0	1
5	0	0	0	0	1	0	0	0	0	0	0	0	1	0	0	1
10	0	0	0	0	0	1	0	0	0	0	0	0	1	0	0	0
4	0	0	0	0	0	1	0	0	0	0	0	0	1	0	0	0
9	0	0	0	0	0	0	1	0	0	0	0	0	0	1	1	0
5	0	0	0	0	0	0	1	0	0	0	0	0	0	1	1	0
9	0	0	0	0	0	0	0	1	0	0	0	0	0	1	0	1
5	0	0	0	0	0	0	0	1	0	0	0	0	0	1	0	1
5	0	0	0	0	0	0	0	0	1	0	0	0	0	1	0	0
3	0	0	0	0	0	0	0	0	1	0	0	0	0	1	0	0
3	0	0	0	0	0	0	0	0	0	1	0	0	0	0	1	0
1	0	0	0	0	0	0	0	0	0	1	0	0	0	0	1	0
9	0	0	0	0	0	0	0	0	0	0	1	0	0	0	0	1
7	0	0	0	0	0	0	0	0	0	0	1	0	0	0	0	1
10	0	0	0	0	0	0	0	0	0	0	0	0	0	0	0	0
6	0	0	0	0	0	0	0	0	0	0	0	0	0	0	0	0

Using the four models (Models 1-4), the portion of the summary table for regression can be used directly. The portions of interest, taken directly from the printout, are reported in Table 8.4.

TABLE 8.4

VALUES FOUND FROM THE REGRESSION ANALYSES

	df	SS	R^2
Model 1			
Attributable to Regression	11	312	.77228
Deviation from Regression	12	92	.22772
Total Sum of Squares	23	404	
Model 2 (Rows)			
Attributable to Regression	3	204	.50495
Model 3 (Columns)			
Attributable to Regression	2	16	.03960
Model 4 (Rows & Columns)			
Attributable to Regression	5	220	.54455

The data from Table 8.4 can be put into a summary table. There are four sources of variation of interest in a two-way analysis of variance: rows, columns, interaction (among rows and columns) and the within group variation. The sum of squares for rows can be found directly from Model 2 as the value for attributable to regression and is 204. The sum of squares for columns can be found directly from Model 3 as the value for attributable to regression and is 16. The sum of squares within is equal to the deviation from regression for Model 1 and is 92. The interaction can be found as the difference in sum of squares between the attributable to regression for Model 1 and the attributable to regression for Model 4: 312 - 220 = 92.

Also, the degrees of freedom are necessary for each source of variation. The degrees of freedom for rows is the number of rows minus one (r - 1); the degrees of freedom for columns is the number of columns minus one (c - 1); the degrees of freedom for interaction is the product of the degrees of freedom for rows and columns [(r - 1)(c - 1)] ; the total degrees of freedom are the total number of subjects minus one (N - 1).

All of the information for the data in Table 8.4 can be put into a summary table. See Table 8.5.

TABLE 8.5

SUMMARY TABLE FOR DATA FOR METHOD OF TEACHING X TYPE OF HOMEWORK

Source of Variation	df	SS	MS
Rows	3	204.00	68.00
Columns	2	16.00	8.00
Interaction	6	92.00	15.33
Within	12	92.00	7.67
Total	23	404.00	

At least two questions are likely to surface at this point. Just what is interaction? and, what do you do with the data after constructing the summary table? The next two sections are attempts to answer those questions.

8.5 Interaction

Briefly, interaction can be thought of as the variation due to the cells after the effects of the rows and columns have been eliminated. Alternatively, interaction can be thought of as the effect upon the cells of being in their particular treatment combinations. As can be determined from the previous calculations, the interaction is the difference in the complete twelve group model and a combined model that includes row and column information. This process answers the question, what is left over after you take out the effect of the rows and columns?

8.6 Interpreting the Data from a Two-Way Analysis of Variance

First, a "traditional" interpretation is given, and then criticized (some would say the straw man is knocked over).

In a traditional approach, the interaction is tested first. If the interaction is non-significant, then the row effect and column effect (main effects) are tested. If the interaction effect is significant, then, presumably the main effects are not particularly relevant, and the "simple" effects might be investigated. By "simple" effects is usually meant testing among the means by multiple comparison procedures, with the comparison often restricted within the same row or same column (though not necessarily).

To run these tests (F tests) an F value can be formed by testing the mean square for each effect against the MS_W term.

The test for interaction is:

$$F = \frac{MS_{RC}}{MS_W} = \frac{15.33}{7.67} = 2.00.$$

With degrees of freedom 6 and 12, this result is non-significant at the .05 level, since 2.00 is less than the tabled value of 3.00. The effect for rows is given by:

$F = \frac{MS_R}{MS_W} = \frac{8.00}{7.67} = 1.04$, which is non-significant at the .05 degrees of freedom 3 and 12, since 1.04 is less than 3.49.

The effect for columns is given by:

$F = \frac{MS_C}{MS_W} = \frac{68.00}{7.67} = 8.87$, which is significant at both the .05 and .01 levels with 2 and 12 degrees of freedom, since 8.87 is larger than both 3.88 and 6.93 (Typically, only one significance level would be reported).

There are two criticisms to this "typical," or "traditional" approach. First, by testing the interaction, and then proceeding depending upon the outcome of this test, the reporting of main effects will occur only when the interaction effect is non-significant. Clearly, this demands an argument from non-significance, a rather novel approach. Additionally, one must assume that any interaction is extrinsic (that is, within the bounds of sampling error). If one is willing to assume the non-existence of intrinsic interaction (that is, "real" interaction) then one may wonder why someone would test for it; particularly, it seems at least interesting that a researcher would argue from non-significance when earlier the same researcher might have claimed that if a t-test showed no significant difference, that is no conclusive evidence that the two means are equal; rather, the researcher was simply unable to show the two means were unequal. Thus, the criticism here is in regard to the argument from non-significance for the test of interaction.

The second criticism is made in regard to error rate. The sequential testing implied here will not retain an experimentwise error rate. If three sequential tests are involved with independent tests, the experimentwise error rate would be $1 - (1 - \alpha)^3$ rather than α. If the apparent level is the .05 level, then the experimentwise error rate is .142625. If an experimentwise error rate is to be maintained, then to have significance at the .05 level, the apparent level should be approximately the .017 level. Empirically, the experiment could be run at the .01 level and reported at the .05 level. This approach would be a little conservative, however. Because the interpretation given here is somewhat different from the usual applied statistics texts, a few additional comments should be made. Most researchers would evaluate each F value independently; that is, they would use a 5% level for each statement. This approach is not incorrect in a statistical sense, and can be used if the researcher understands the limitations involved. If each F value is tested against the F distribution independently at the 5% level, then the chance of any statement being incorrectly rejected is 5%. Because there are three statements being tested, there is a .142625 chance of reporting one or more erroneous rejections in the experiment. Thus, if a person tests each F value against the F distribution at a given level, and reports the experiment at that level, he should understand that he is using a per comparison error rate rather than an experimentwise error rate.

8.7 Treatments X Levels Design

The treatments X levels design is computationally identical to the factoral design. One of the "factors" in a treatments X levels design is usually a control variable in levels. For example, the experiment given in Table 8.2 might be reconceptualized. The researcher might feel that the method of teaching is no longer of experimental interest, but he may wish to test the four types of homework in regard to ability level. He may then get a new group of subjects and classify them first into levels (high, middle, low) and then, within levels, randomly assign an equal number to each type of homework, and then the two-way analysis of variance. Usually, there is little interest in the level effect. Thus, only the interaction effect and type of homework effect would be tested.

8.8 An Alternative Formulation for Model 1

The linear model given for Model 1 was a model that ignored row and column information, and viewed the problem as one that contained twelve groups. An alternative formulation (Model 1a) is:

$$Y = b_0 + b_{12}X_{12} + b_{13}X_{13} + b_{14}X_{14} + b_{15}X_{15} + b_{16}X_{16} + b_{17}X_{17} + b_{18}X_{18} + b_{19}X_{19} + b_{20}X_{20} + b_{21}X_{21} + b_{22}X_{22} + e_1, \quad (8.5)$$

where

b_0 = the Y-intercept (and equal to the mean of group 12),

X_{12} - X_{16} = as defined previously,

X_{17} = the <u>product</u> of X_{12} times X_{15} ($X_{12} \cdot X_{15}$),

$X_{18} = X_{12} \cdot X_{16}$,

$X_{19} = X_{13} \cdot X_{15}$,

$X_{20} = X_{13} \cdot X_{16}$,

$X_{21} = X_{14} \cdot X_{15}$,

$X_{22} = X_{14} \cdot X_{16}$,

b_{12} - b_{22} = are regression coefficients corresponding to X_{12} - X_{22}, and

e_1 = the error in prediction with this model.

Both Model 1 and Model 1a can be referred to as <u>full models</u>. It can be seen that X_{12} - X_{14} impart row information, X_{15} - X_{16} impart column information, and X_{17} - X_{22} report the product of row and column information. Thus, interaction is the difference between the full model and the model that does not include the product of row and column information.

8.9. Other Regression Formulations of the Two-Way Analysis of Variance

Bottenberg and Ward (1963) and Jennings (1967) present a much different model conceptually; to the casual reader, it would seem the approach given here and the regression approach given in Bottenberg and Ward and Jennings would end up with very different results. Basically, the approaches of the just mentioned writers involves the development of several models. First, a full model is developed, and then, restrictions are made on the regression coefficients to develop <u>restricted</u> models. While the interested reader is encouraged to examine these other sources, the reader is assured that the approach given in this chapter, the approaches of Bottenberg and Ward, Jennings and the more usual two-way analysis of variance found in most applied statistics texts yield the same final summary table.

8.10 Summary

A regression approach to the two-way analysis of variance design is given. The two-way factoral design allows for two classification schemes, rather than one. For example, the researcher may cross-classify sex and colleges within a university, and then test for difference on some criterion, such as ACT scores. Care must be taken in a traditional analysis to be sure the proportionality requirement is satisfied. When one of the ways of classification represents levels of some factor, the two-way factoral design is usually called a treatments X levels design.

EXERCISES

8.1 Given the following set of data, complete the analysis, and construct a summary table.

ACT Scores

Sex	Arts and Sciences	Education	Engineering
Male	20	21	21
	18	17	22
	18	19	16
	16	14	18
	21	12	23
	22	26	
	24	28	
	28	21	
	29	14	
	16	15	
	18		
	13		
	15		
	18		
	17		
Female	19	23	27
	17	29	24
	17	21	22
	16	17	
	18	15	
	27	13	
	14		
	15		
	16		

a) Test the interaction effect for significance. How does this result effect the main effect tests?

b) Test both main effects for significance and interpret.

8.2 Given the following set of data, complete the analysis, and construct a summary table.

Statistics Test Scores

	Degree Sought	
Anxiety Level	Master's	Doctor's
High	35	32
	31	37
	28	30
	16	29
	25	17
Middle	48	43
	42	38
	31	37
	28	32
	31	40
Low	30	43
	27	38
	31	49
	20	40
	22	35

a) Test the interaction for significance.

b) Even though this is a treatments X levels design, both main effects are likely to be of interest. Test both main effects.

CHAPTER NINE

TWO-WAY ANALYSIS OF VARIANCE WITH DISPROPORTIONATE CELL FREQUENCIES

9.1 Introduction

One of the requirements for a two-way analysis of variance given in Chapter Eight was that the cell frequencies must be proportional row to row and column to column. A natural question arises, "So what happens if they're not proportional?" The answer to that question depends very much upon the orientation of the researcher and/or statistician.

First, consider the following situation: a researcher wants to do research regarding students in four different colleges (arts and sciences, education, engineering and nursing) and wants to use sex as a second factor. The distribution of students in the university where the researcher is conducting his study are as follows:

TABLE 9.1

DISTRIBUTION OF STUDENTS BY COLLEGE AND SEX

	Arts and Sciences	Education	Engineering	Nursing
Male	1817	806	417	12
Female	1183	994	13	118

The approaches to analyzing data on subjects distributed as in Table 9.1 are various. There are three general kinds of solutions; solutions where proportionality is forced, approximate solutions and full regression solutions.

9.2 Solutions where Proportionality is Forced

The two more common data forcing solutions are discarding data and estimating "missing data." For data distributed as in Table 9.1, the data forcing methods would border on the ludicrous, and would have only one saving grace. If data were to be discarded, then 404 of the 417 male engineers would have to be randomly thrown out; likewise, 106 of the 118 female nursing students would have to be discarded. A considerable number of students in the other two colleges would also have to be discarded. The virtue of discarding data to reach proportionality is that the college effect and the sex effect are then independent of one another. Clearly, reducing the sample as much as is indicated would seem to be too costly in terms of the total experiment; additionally, college and sex are not normally independent; to make them so for the present analysis might seem indefensible.

The second data forcing method is to estimate "missing" data. Cochran and Cox (1957) describe the technique. For reasons not dissimilar to the line of reasoning given with the discarding of data, estimating missing data would be ineffectual for the college X sex problem.

9.3 The Approximate Solutions

Several approximate solutions have been described. The method of unweighted means has been quite popular, and is described by Walker and Lev (1953); Scheffé (1959) and Glass and Stanley (1970).

A second approximate solution is the method of expected cell frequencies due to Snedecor and Cox (1935) and described more recently by Myers (1966). A third approximate solution is the method of weighted means described in detail by Steinhorst and Miller (1969).

The three approximate solutions have in common a desire to yield a method that achieves an analysis that would be similar to the usual two-way analysis of variance and given a useful measure of interaction. All three methods effectively achieve proportionality so that the effects are independent of one another; the measure of interaction is actually an exact solution for the method of weighted means and the method of unweighted means.

9.4 The Exact Solutions

One of the difficulties with the statement, "If there are disproportionate cell frequencies in a two-way analysis of variance, then a full regression, or least squares, solution should be used," is that there is more than one regression solution. The different solutions are due to different considerations in regard to an experiment. Three different solutions are described here; they are by no means an exhaustive list of the regression solutions.

The data in Table 9.2 are used in the following sections for the analysis of disproportionate cell frequencies for a two-way analysis of variance.

TABLE 9.2

DATA FOR DISPROPORTIONATE TWO-WAY ANALYSIS OF VARIANCE

Effect	B_1	B_2	B_3
A_1	8 6 4	1 1	6 2
A_2	10	7 5 4 4 3	10 9 7 5 4

9.5 The Method of Fitting Constants

The most commonly described least squares solution for disproportionate cell frequencies for a two-way analysis of variance is the method of fitting constants. The method is described in the standard texts (Winer, 1971; Rao, 1965; Scheffe, 1959; Anderson and Bancroft, 1952). This solution can be obtained from the same four selections given in Chapter Eight. This method involves adjusting the A (row) effect for the B (column) effect, adjusting the B effect for the A effect, and adjusting the AB (interaction) effect for both the A and B effects.

To accomplish this analysis, it is useful to conceptualize several linear models. The full model for this situation can be written:

$$Y = \mu + \alpha_i + \beta_j + \alpha\beta_{ij} + e, \qquad (9.1)$$

where μ is the grand mean, the α_i are deviations of the row means from the grand mean, the β_j are deviations of the column means from the grand mean, the $\alpha\beta_{ij}$ are deviations of the cell means from the row and column effects and e is the error in prediction.

For the data in Table 9.2, a full model (Model 1) can be developed that is the direct application of equation 9.1:

$$Y = b_0 + b_1X_1 + b_2X_2 + b_3X_3 + b_4X_4 + b_5X_5 + e_1, \qquad (9.2)$$

where

X_1 = 1 if the score is from a member in row 1; 0 otherwise,

X_2 = 1 if the score is from a member in column 1; 0 otherwise,

X_3 = 1 if the score is from a member in column 2; 0 otherwise,

$X_4 = X_1 \cdot X_2$ = 1 if the score is from a member in row 1 and column 1; 0 otherwise,

$X_5 = X_1 \cdot X_3$ = 1 if the score is from a member in row 1 and column 2; 0 otherwise,

b_0 = the Y-intercept for Model 1 (and is equal to the mean of the group in row 2, column 3),

$b_1 - b_5$ = are the regression coefficients for $X_1 - X_5$; and

e_1 = the error in prediction with Model 1.

There are alternative ways of expressing the full model that will yield the same general solution. One useful approach is to define a cell model for the full model as follows:

$$Y = b_0 + b_6X_6 + b_7X_7 + b_8X_8 + b_9X_9 + b_{10}X_{10} + e_1, \qquad (9.3)$$

where

X_6 = 1 if the score is from a member in row 1 and column 1; 0 otherwise,

X_7 = 1 if the score is from a member in row 1 and column 2; 0 otherwise,

X_8 = 1 if the score is from a member in row 1 and column 3; 0 otherwise,

X_9 = 1 if the score is from a member in row 2 and column 1; 0 otherwise,

X_{10} = 1 if the score is from a member in row 2 and column 2; 0 otherwise,

b_0 = the Y-intercept for this model (and is equal to the mean of the group in row 2, column 3),

$b_6 - b_{10}$ = are regression coefficients for $X_6 - X_{10}$, and

e_1 = the error in prediction with this model.

The results for this model will yield the same solution as Model 1; equation 9.3 is in fact the complete one-way layout of all six cells, similar to Model 1 in Chapter Eight.

A model (Model 2) can be defined for the A effect for the data in Table 9.2:

$$Y = b_0 + b_1X_1 + e_2, \qquad (9.4)$$

where

X_1 = 1 if the score is from a member in row 1; and 0 otherwise,

b_0 = the Y-intercept for Model 1 (and is equal to the mean of row 2),

b_1 = the regression coefficient for X_1; and

e_2 = the error in prediction with Model 2.

A model (Model 3) can also be defined for the B effect:

$$Y = b_0 + b_2X_2 + b_3X_3 + e_3, \qquad (9.5)$$

where

X_2 = 1 if the score is from a member in column 1; and 0 otherwise,

X_3 = 1 if the score is from a member in column 2; and 0 otherwise,

b_0 = the Y-intercept for Model 3 (and is equal to the mean of column 3),

$b_2 - b_3$ = are regression coefficients for $X_2 - X_3$; and

e_3 = the error in prediction with Model 3.

Finally, a model (Model 4) can be developed for the combined A and B effects:

$$Y = b_0 + b_1X_1 + b_2X_2 + b_3X_3 + e_4, \qquad (9.6)$$

where

X_1 = 1 if the score is from a member in row 1; 0 otherwise,

X_2 = 1 if the score is from a member in column 1; 0 otherwise,

X_3 = 1 if the score is from a member in column 2; 0 otherwise,

b_0 = the Y-intercept for Model 4 (and is equal to the mean of the group in row 2 and column 3),

b_1 - b_3 = are the regression coefficients for X_1 - X_3; and

e_4 = the error in prediction with Model 4.

b_1, b_2 and b_3 will, in general, be different for equations 9.2, 9.4, 9.5 and 9.6.

The information from the four models can be summarized (See Table 9.3).

TABLE 9.3

REGRESSION FORMULATION FOR THE TWO-WAY ANALYSIS OF VARIANCE

Y	X_1	X_2	X_3	X_4	X_5
8	1	1	0	1	0
6	1	1	0	1	0
4	1	1	0	1	0
1	1	0	1	0	1
1	1	0	1	0	1
6	1	0	0	0	0
2	1	0	0	0	0
10	0	1	0	0	0
7	0	0	1	0	0
5	0	0	1	0	0
4	0	0	1	0	0
4	0	0	1	0	0
3	0	0	1	0	0
10	0	0	0	0	0
9	0	0	0	0	0
7	0	0	0	0	0
5	0	0	0	0	0
4	0	0	0	0	0

The values from the regression program that are useful for completing the analysis of variance are the sum of squares attributable to regression for Models 1, 2, 3 and 4, and the sum of squares for deviation from regression for Model 1. The R^2 values are also included in Table 9.4. The total sum of squares is available from all four models.

TABLE 9.4

VALUES FOUND FROM THE REGRESSION ANALYSES

	df	SS	R^2
Model 1 (Full Model)			
Attributable to Regression	5	80.80	.61212
Deviation from Regression	12	51.20	
Total Sum of Squares	17	132.00	
Model 2 (A effect)			
Attributable to Regression	1	20.36	.15427
Model 3 (B effect)			
Attributable to Regression	2	37.43	.28355
Model 4 (Combined A & B effects)			
Attributable to Regression		80.25	.60796

The A effect for the method of fitting constants is the difference between the sum of squares for attributable to regression for Model 4 and Model 3;

$$SS_A = 80.25 - 37.43 = 42.82.$$

Essentially, this process amounts to finding that part of the A effect that is independent of the B effect.

The B effect for this method is the difference between the sum of squares for attributable to regression for Model 4 and Model 2;

$$SS_B = 80.25 - 20.36 = 59.89.$$

Similarly, this second calculation yields that part of the B effect that is independent of the A effect.

And finally, the interaction is found as the difference between Model 1 and Model 4;

$SS_{AB} = 80.80 - 80.25 = .55$. Thus, the effect found in this manner is the AB effect independent of the A and B effects.

The sum of squares within is equal to the deviation from regression for Model 1.

This analysis can be summarized in terms of equation 9.1 and in yerms of the R^2 values:

Sources of Variation	df	SS
A	a - 1	$SS_T\left[R^2(\alpha_i, \beta_j) - R^2(\beta_j)\right]$
B	b - 1	$SS_T\left[R^2(\alpha_i, \beta_j) - R^2(\alpha_j)\right]$
AB	(a - 1)(b - 1)	$SS_T\left[R^2(\alpha_i, \beta_j, \alpha\beta_{ij} - R^2(\alpha_i, \beta_j)\right]$
Within	N - ab	$SS_T\left[1 - R^2(\alpha_i, \beta_j, \alpha\beta_{ij})\right]$
Total	N - 1	SS_T

This information for the data in Table 9.3 can be put into a summary table and is found in Table 9.5.

TABLE 9.5

SUMMARY TABLE FOR THE METHOD OF FITTING CONSTANTS

Source of Variation	df	SS	MS	F
A	1	42.82	42.82	10.03
B	2	59.89	29.95	7.01
AB	2	.55	.28	.07
Within	12	51.20	4.27	

The method of fitting constants is not a partitioning model. That is, if the sum of squares are totaled, they do not equal the total sum of squares of 132.00 (If the sum of squares are totaled for the method of fitting constants, the sum is 154.46).

9.6 The Hierarchical Model

The hierarchical model (Cohen, 1968) is a method similar to the method of fitting constants. With this approach, a researcher is required to order the variables in relation to their interest. For example, a researcher may be most interested in the A, or row effect, less interested in the B, or column effect, and have little interest in the interaction effect. With this approach, each effect is adjusted only for those effects preceding it in the ordering. Thus, the A effect is found directly, the B effect is adjusted for the A effect, and the AB effect is adjusted for both the A effect and the B effect. Unlike the previous model, this model is additive in the sense that the sum $SS_A + SS_B + SS_{AB} + SS_w$ is equal to SS_T.

The hierarchical model analysis can also be summarized in terms of equation 9.1 and the R^2 values:

Source of Variation	df	SS
A	a - 1	$SS_T \left[R^2(\alpha_i)\right]$
B	b - 1	$SS_T \left[R^2(\alpha_i, \beta_j) - R^2(\alpha_i)\right]$
AB	(a - 1)(b - 1)	$SS_T \left[R^2(\alpha_i, \beta_j, \alpha\beta_{ij}) - R^2(\alpha_i, \beta_j)\right]$
Within	N - ab	$SS_T \left[1 - R^2(\alpha_i, \beta_j, \alpha\beta_{ij})\right]$
Total	N - 1	SS_T

The values for SS_A, SS_B and SS_w can be found from Table 9.4:

$SS_A = 20.36$, the unadjusted A effect;

$SS_B = 80.25 - 20.36 = 59.89$, that part of B independent of A;

$SS_{AB} = 80.80 - 80.25 = .55$, as previously,

and

$SS_w = 51.20.$

These values are placed in a usual summary table (see Table 9.6.).

TABLE 9.6

SUMMARY TABLE FOR THE HIERARCHICAL MODEL

Source of Variation	df	SS	MS	F
A	1	20.36	20.36	4.77
B	2	59.89	29.95	7.01
AB	2	.55	.28	.07
Within	12	51.20	4.27	
Total	17	132.00		

The results from this analysis are identical to the fitting constants method except for the SS_A term. The interpretation would be somewhat different however, because of the decrease in size of the SS_A term. If, on the other hand, the researcher had chosen his order of experimental interest as B, A, AB, then the F values for the A effect and the AB effect would be unchanged from the fitting constants method, but the B effect would be smaller.

9.7 The Unadjusted Main Effects Method

A solution similar to the two previous least squares solutions can be called the unadjusted main effects method. Using this approach, both the A and B effects are found directly, with the interaction found in the same manner as the method of fitting constants and the hierarchical model. The error term (mean square within) is of course the same. The unadjusted main effects method can also be summarized in terms of equation 9.1 and the R^2 values:

Source of Variation	df	SS
A	a - 1	$SS_T\left[R^2(\alpha_i)\right]$
B	b - 1	$SS_T\left[R^2(\beta_j)\right]$
AB	(a - 1)(b - 1)	$SS_T\left[R^2(\alpha_i, \beta_j, \alpha\beta_{ij}) - R^2(\alpha_i, \beta_j)\right]$
Within	N - ab	$SS_T\left[1 - R^2(\alpha_i, \beta_j, \alpha\beta_{ij})\right]$.
Total	N - 1	SS_T

The values for SS_A, SS_B, SS_{AB}, and SS_W can be found from Table 9.4:

SS_A = 20.36, the unadjusted A effect;

SS_B = 37.43, the unadjusted B effect;

SS_{AB} = 80.80 - 80.25 = .55, as previously;

and

SS_W = 51.20.

Table 9.7 contains the unadjusted main effects method analysis.

TABLE 9.7

SUMMARY TABLE FOR THE UNADJUSTED MAIN EFFECTS METHOD

Source of Variation	df	SS	MS	F
A	1	20.36	20.36	4.77
B	2	37.43	18.72	4.38
AB	2	.55	.28	.07
Within	12	51.20	4.27	

The unadjusted main effects method bears a striking resemblance to the usual analysis of variance for proportional cell frequencies. Had the usual analysis of variance technique been employed, the results for the A and B effects would be identical to the unadjusted main effects method. The interaction for the usual analysis of variance found as a residual is 23.01 rather than .55. What appears to be a trivial interaction would have been greatly over-estimated by the analysis of variance method. If the sum of squares were totaled for Table 9.7, the total is less than 132.00 (the total for Table 9.7 is actually 109.54). The unadjusted main effects method yields the same values as the solution proposed by Jennings (1967). That Jennings' approach and the unadjusted main effects method yield the same results was shown by Halldorson (1969). The use of the term "main effect" here is meant the comparison between the levels of a factor.

9.8 Relationship of the Three Regression Solutions

While Tables 9.5, 9.6, and 9.7 have been generated so that they appear similar to the usual analysis of variance tables, the results could have as easily been conceptualized in terms of the R^2 values. If it is remembered that the ease of computation with the proportional case for a two-way fixed effects solution is due to the independence of the A effect, the B effect, and the AB effect, it can be seen how a slightly different rationale will allow different solutions. Thus, the A and B effects for the unadjusted main effects are found directly (that is, neither main effect is partialled from the other). With the hierarchical solution, the more important of the A and B effects (more important as defined by the researcher) is found directly. If the A effect was considered more important, then the A effect for the hierarchical model would be identical to the A effect for the unadjusted main effects method. However, in the hierarchical model, only the portion of the B effect independent of the A effect is found. For the fitting constants method, both the A and B effects are adjusted for the other effect. If the data were proportional, on the other hand, all three methods would yield the same solution. The interaction effect is the same in all three models.

In choosing between the three methods for a solution, the following points would seem relevant:

1) if one effect (either A or B) is clearly of more interest than the other effect, then the hierarchical model would be useful;
2) if the interest is in the independent portion of an effect, the fitting constants method would be appropriate;
3) the method of unadjusted main effects is slightly easier to calculate and is more similar computationally to the usual analysis of variance procedure;
4) the method of unadjusted main effects does <u>not</u> yield the independent portions of an effect, nor is the first effect found in the hierarchical model independent;
5) only the hierarchical solution will total to SS_T, that is, the method of fitting constants and the method of unadjusted main effects are not partitioning models;
6) the interaction effect is identical in all three procedures; and
7) if the data is proportional, all three methods will yield the same solution.

It should be evident that no one method will always be preferred over the other two; rather, the research situation should dictate the choice of the solution for disproportionate cell frequencies in a two-way fixed effects analysis.

9.9 Summary

Of the three general types of methods considered, the least squares solutions would seem to receive greater emphasis with the availability of computers. The data forcing (forced proportionality) methods and approximate solutions would likely more often be used at the beginning and intermediate stages of research, with the more sophisticated least squares solutions being employed at the end stage. The data forcing methods might continue in usage for quite some time because of the distastefulness of disproportionality to some researchers. Because the approximation methods have generally been concerned with estimating the method of fitting constants, this least squares solution would seem to have an increased acceptance with the increasing availability of computers. This method has been considered to be the analog to usual analysis of variance procedure, but is directly applicable when disproportionality exists.

Williams (1972a) has compared the three approximate solutions and the three exact solutions using the same data points so that the six methods can be contrasted, both as to the process and as to the final result. Other least squares solutions have been tried beyond those examined herein. Overall and Spiegel (1969) discuss a model they termed the general linear model analysis. In this procedure each effect is adjusted for every other effect. While the model gave comparable results to the other methods (including the usual analysis of variance) in the equal cells case, the method failed for the proportional case, leading Overall and Spiegel to dismiss the model as an analog to the analysis of variance.

EXERCISES

9.1 Consider the following problem:

		B effect			
		B_1	B_2	B_3	B_4
A effect	A_1	8	12	9	13
		6	17	9	18
			12	8	12
				12	11
				14	11
				11	
	A_2	3	6	5	17
		4	8	7	12
		5	6	2	10
		5	3		10
		2	3		
		5	9		

a) Complete and analysis of variance using the fitting of constants method.
b) Complete the analysis of variance using the hierarchical method.
c) Complete the analysis of variance using the unadjusted main effects method.

9.2 Re-do problem 8.1,

a) using the fitting of constants method;
b) using the hierarchical method; and
c) using the unadjusted main effects method.

CHAPTER TEN

STEPWISE AND SETWISE REGRESSION ANALYSIS

10.1 Introduction

Two closely related techniques are described in this chapter. The stepwise regression technique is first considered, wherein a predictive system is formed by dropping one variable at a time, until only one variable remains in the system. A second method is the setwise regression solution, which works in the same way as the stepwise solution, except that sets of variables are included, rather than using only single variables.

10.2 Stepwise Regression Analysis

A useful descriptive multiple linear regression technique is stepwise regression analysis. There are actually several stepwise regression schemes (see, for example, Draper and Smith, 1966), however, the stepwise backward technique illustrates one effective approach to the stepwise process.

The stepwise backward process begins with k predictor variables. First, a full model is developed with all k variables. Then, in k - 1 additional steps, one predictor is dropped at each step, until only one variable remains. The researcher is thus able to assess which variables are contributing the most to the prediction of the criterion. The variable to be dropped at each step is chosen on the basis of allowing the smallest possible loss in the multiple correlation coefficient. The variable with the smallest computed t value (smallest in absolute value) is dropped at each step. Actually, the t value is a test of significance of each regression coefficient for each model. Strictly speaking, whenever more than one regression coefficient is involved, the regression coefficients are called partial regression coefficients, and the t test is a test of whether the partial regression coefficient is significantly different from zero. The t test is not exactly the same as the usual t test, because several t tests are involved simultaneously in regard to the same criterion. Some of the same considerations are involved as are found in considerations regarding multiple comparisons.

A stepwise regression analysis was employed by Williams, Harlow and Gab (1970) when they were trying to assess success of doctoral students at the University of North Dakota (UND). They used 15 predictor variables, with the criterion being whether or not the student graduated from the doctoral program. The criterion was binary coded with graduated = 1 and not-graduated = 0. The 15 predictor variables were:

1. Area of concentration (either teacher education = 1, or administration = 0),
2. Years between bachelor's degree and doctoral admission,
3. Years between master's degree and doctoral admission,
4. Whether or not master's degree was from UND (Yes = 1, No = 0),
5. Age at admission,
6. Accumulative grade point average (GPA) for bachelor's degree,
7. Accumulative GPA for master's degree,
8. Number of courses in education before starting doctoral program,
9. Number of years of educational experience,
10. Graduate Record Examination (GRE) Verbal Score,
11. GRE Quantitative score,
12. GRE Advanced Test in Education score,
13. Miller Analogies Test (MAT) score,
14. Degree sought (Ph.D. = 1, Ed.D. = 0), and
15. Sex (Male = 1, Female = 0).

There were 33 graduates and 51 non-graduates involved in the sample. The results of the stepwise regression analysis are shown in Table 10.1.

TABLE 10.1

STEPWISE BACKWARD ELIMINATION PROCEDURE WITH GRADUATED OR NOT-GRADUATED AS THE CRITERION (N = 84)

Step	Variable Eliminated	R	R^2
1	None (Full Model)	.650	.4225
2	Years between master's and doctoral admission	.650	.4225
3	MAT-Test Score	.650	.4225
4	Accumulative GPA for bachelor's degree	.650	.4225
5	Years between bachelor's and doctoral admission	.648	.4199
6	Age	.646	.4173
7	Area of concentration Teacher Ed. or Administration	.641	.4109
8	Accumulative GPA for master's degree	.634	.4020
9	Sex	.629	.3956
10	Number of years of educational experience	.618	.3819
11	Number of courses in education before doctoral admission	.591	.3493
12	Master's degree received from UND	.545	.2970
13	Degree sought Ph.D. or Ed.D.	.499	.2490
14	GRE-Verbal	.435	.1892
15	GRE-Quantitative	.342	.1170
16	GRE-Advanced	----	-----

It can be seen that 6 of the 15 variables can account for most of the accountable variance. Using the 3 GRE scores, the degree sought (Ph.D. or Ed.D.), whether they received the master's degree from UND, and number of courses in education before doctoral admission, account for 38.19 percent of the variance in whether or not a person will graduate. In that a total of 42.25 percent of the variance in the criterion is accounted for by the total predictive system, it might be deduced that these last six variables would be a small but usable set of predictors. The basis for deciding on an optimum predictive system is far from simple. From the previous discussion, the decision was made on the basis of the R^2 term. The reader may wonder why a test involving a probability statement was not made. There are tests that are often applied to the stepwise regression situation (not only the sequential F test) but most of these tests involve using the F distribution in such a way that the probability is being grossly under-estimated. Pragmatically, the drop in the R^2 value seems to be a useful criterion. Rather than rely on the several statistical tests, it seems worthwhile to rely upon the researcher's own judgment for the stepwise situation.

10.3 Setwise Regression Analysis

A technique that is quite similar to the stepwise regression analysis is setwise regression analysis. Williams and Lindem (1971) described the technique and provided a computer solution for the setwise technique.

Instead of using single variables, the researcher is allowed to define sets of variables. While sets can be defined on a logical basis, the use of a setwise procedure would seem mandatory when binary coded variables are included and there are more than two categories involved. In fact, if there are more than two categories involved in the binary coding, then the usual stepwise regression procedure becomes almost meaningless.

Consider the following situation. A researcher is interested in finding the relationships of several variables to alienation in undergraduate students. The variables selected as predictor variables are the following:

1. socioeconomic status of parents;
2. religion: 1 if Catholic, 0 otherwise;
3. religion: 1 if Protestant, 0 otherwise;
4. religion: 1 if Jewish, 0 otherwise;
5. sex: 1 if male, 0 otherwise;
6. class: 1 if freshman, 0 otherwise;

7. class: 1 if sophomore, 0 otherwise;
8. class: 1 if junior, 0 otherwise;
9. grade point average overall;
10. grade point average in major field;
11. a measure of interpersonal aggression;
12. a measure of anomie;
13. a measure of need for people, and
14. a measure of need to help people.

Two variables that seem to be missing are a religion variable and a class variable. Actually, the remaining categories are simply zero-coded. Thus the possibility of "other" or "none" for religion is zero-coded, as is being a senior. It is not important that these two particular variables were zero-coded. For example, the sophomore group could be zero-coded, with the other three classes being binary coded. The results would be unchanged.

With the previous 14 variables, the researcher might have defined seven sets as follows:

Set	Variables
1	1 socioeconomic status
2	2,3,4 religion
3	5 sex
4	6,7,8 class
5	9,10 grade point average
6	11,12 interpersonal aggression and anomie
7	13,14 need for people and need to help people

The setwise procedure drops one set at a time in a stepwise fashion. There will be as many steps as there are sets; for the illustrative example, seven steps would be present. The steps are accomplished by an iterative procedure that allows the R^2 (multiple correlation coefficient squared) term to be maximized at each stage in a backward stepwise procedure. Once a set is discarded, the set is no longer considered at later stages. The computer internally computes the R^2 value for the seven sets; then the R^2 values are found for all possible combinations of 6 sets of variables. Only the highest R^2 value is retained. This process automatically eliminates one set. The procedure is then continued with the remaining six sets until only one set remains.

While the difficulty regarding the use of binary coded predictors has been at least partially solved, other difficulites in regard to the stepwise procedure are also involved in the setwise procedure; additionally, the setwise procedure has a new problem unique to itself.

It has been pointed out that probability levels in the stepwise procedure are usually violated. Further, when k of the N variables have been dropped, the N - k remaining variables are not necessarily the set of N - k variables that would yield the highest R^2 value. These criticisms would also be valid in regard to the setwise procedure. Additionally, the differences in the number of variables in a set will have some effect upon when that set of variables would be dropped. Other things being equal, a set with 6 variables will be retained longer than a set with 3 variables. Norwithstanding these difficulties, if the setwise procedure is judiciously employed by researchers, then additional data analysis power can be obtained.

While the setwise technique has not yet been used extensively, one application was made by Grooters (1971). He was interested in predicting costs per student credit hour in four state colleges. The input data were means by department for 16 variables; nine sets were formed with the 16 variables. Four of the sets were single variables, four sets were logical sets, and one set included a linear dependency among the variables involved. By considering the group of variables with a linear dependency as a set, the linear dependency can be removed by dropping any one variable from the analysis from within the set, and then performing the setwise regression analysis. The results are shown in Table 10.2.

TABLE 10.2

SETWISE REGRESSION ANALYSIS FOR SELECTED VARIABLES
WITH COST OF STUDENT CREDIT HOURS AS A CRITERION

Step	Set Eliminated	R	R^2
1	None	.781	.610
2	Salary	.781	.609
3	College Work (committee assignments, advisees, average hours per week)	.779	.607
4	College and related teaching experience	.777	.602
5	Different preparations	.773	.597
6	Percentage of time allotments (% of time in direct and indirect instruction, % of time in supplementary instruction, % of time in research, and % of time in administrative service)	.767	.588
7	Rank and degree	.750	.562
8	Percentage of instructional time spent on producing upper division credits	.727	.528
9	Hours of outside of school activity	.634	.402
10	Contact hours and credit hours	-	-

From Table 10.2 it can be seen that the most important set for predicting instructional salary costs is the number of contact hours and number of credit hours taught by the typical member of a department. The next most important set is the single variable of the number of hours of outside of school activity (both paid and unpaid). The first set dropped was the mean salary for the various departments; this reflects a situation where the salaries do not vary too much from department to department and from college to college.

10.4 The Unique Contribution of a Variable or a Set of Variables

When working with a predictive system, interest is sometimes focused on such questions as, "Given the existing data, how much new information (predictability) is added by using another predictor (or set of predictors?)" One approach to this problem is the concept of unique contributions, which was shown with a detailed analysis by Ward and Hook (1962). To find the unique contribution of a variable, first a full model is defined and a multiple linear regression is executed with the full model; a multiple correlation for the full model (R_{FM}) is routinely printed out. If R^2_{FM} is not printed out, then the R_{FM} can be squared. Then, the variable (or set of variables) are dropped from the analysis; this second model is called a restricted model with a corresponding multiple correlation squared (R^2_{RM}). The unique contribution for the dropped variable is then

$$\text{Unique Contribution} = R^2_{FM} - R^2_{RM}. \qquad (10.1)$$

The unique contribution can be thought of as the proportion of the variance uniquely attributable to a variable (or set of variables) in a given group of predictors.

The drop of accountable variance from R^2_{FM} to R^2_{RM} (or unique contribution) can be tested to see if there is a significant loss in information.

The test is given by

$$F = \frac{(R^2_{FM} - R^2_{RM})/k}{(1 - R^2_{FM})/N - k - 1}, \qquad (10.2)$$

where k is the number of variables in the dropped set. If a single variable is involved, k = 1. The degrees of freedom are k and N - k - 1.

While the concept of the unique contribution of a variable is quite straightforward, it has given rise to considerable controversy. To review adequately that controversy, several chapters could easily be written. There are at least two salient points to that controversy. First, it is possible for a predictor (or set of predictors) to "account" for a negative variance. It is also possible for a predictor (but usually a set of predictors) to exceed the R^2_{FM} value. A negative accounting of variance does not have a nice intuitive interpretation. Jordan (1971) had several examples of a negative accounting of variance, and did not try to interpret the "negative" variance accounted for in his data.

The second salient point is that if all the unique contributions for each variable are added, the sum would rarely total 100% of the accounted variance. This is because, with real data, variables are rarely mutually independent of one another. If the data are independent of one another, as occurs in the analyses of variances described in Chapter Eight, then the term "orthogonal" (meaning independent) is applied. Bottenberg and Ward (1963), Ward (1969), and Creager (1971) are advocates of the unique (or independent) contribution approach. Criticisms of the approach are made by Tukey (1954) and Werts (1970). Darlington (1968) discusses the issue with several contrasting approaches to assessing the contribution of a variable.

10.5 Summary

Two related stepwise techniques are described in this chapter. One of the more common stepwise techniques is the stepwise backward regression. The stepwise backward technique begins with a full model that contains all of the predictor variables. The predictor variables are then dropped one at a time, with the variable being eliminated at any step being the variable that contributes least to the prediction of the criterion at that step. The second stepwise technique is called setwise regression. The setwise technique works in the same manner as the stepwise technique, except that it works with sets of variables rather than being concerned with single variables only.

The last regression concept considered in this chapter is the concept of the unique contribution of a predictor variable. The unique contribution of a variable is the difference between the R^2 value for the full model and the R^2 value for a restricted model that does not include the variable in question

$$(R^2_{FM} - R^2_{RM}). \qquad (10.1)$$

EXERCISES

10.1 Find the unique contribution of the intelligence scores for the data in Table 3.1 and 3.2 and test for significance (using equation 10.2).

10.2 Find the unique contribution of the manual dexterity scores for the data in Tables 3.1 and 3.2 and test for significance.

(10.1) $r_{x_1 Y} = .73049 = R_{(RM)} \Rightarrow R^2_{(RM)} = .5336156$

$R_{(FM)} = .83961 = R_{(FM)} \Rightarrow R^2_{(FM)} = .7049449$

The unique contribution of Int. Sc

$R^2_{(FM)} - R^2_{(R,M)} = .1713293 = 0.$

$F = \frac{R^2_{FM} - R^2_{RM}}{1 - R^2_{(FM)}} = \frac{.1713293}{1 - .7049449} = \frac{.1713293}{.2950551} = 0.580668$

10.2 $r_{x_2 Y} = .78775 = R_{(RM)} \Rightarrow R^2_{(RM)} = .6205500$

$R_{(FM)} = .83961 = R_{(FM)} \Rightarrow R_{(FM)} = .7049449$

The contribution of Dexter

$.7049449 - .6205500 = .0843$

$R^2_{(FM)} - R^2_{(RM)} = 0.08$

$F = \frac{.0843949}{.2950551} = .2860330$

CHAPTER ELEVEN

THE ANALYSIS OF COVARIANCE

11.1 Introduction

An effective experimental approach is to implement a "statistical" control. That is, the experimenter may wish to remove the effect of a concommitant variable. For example, three groups might be involved in an experiment wherein they were randomly assigned to their respective groups; because there is a concern that another variable, such as intelligence may be highly related to success on the criterion, it is possible to "covary" the intelligence variable (provided the measure of intelligence proceeds the experiment, so that the covariate is not contaminated by the experiment itself). If the covariate is highly related to the criterion, then a considerable reduction can be made in the error variance, allowing a more precise experiment to take place.

In many situations, a pre-test can be given, before an experiment takes place, and a post-test occurs at the conclusion of the experiment. Here, the pre-test can serve as the covariate; also, the pre-test--post-test situation can be viewed as a measure of change.

11.2 The Analysis of Covariance with Pre-Testing

The analysis of covariance takes into account the correlation between the pre-test and the post-test. More specifically, it is helpful to look at the process of the analysis of covariance as it can be generated through the use of linear models. Before the linear models are developed, it is useful to set forth a concrete example. Suppose 15 students are assigned at random to three different methods of learning beginning typewriting. The 15 students begin in the same classroom for two weeks before they are assigned into the three different methods. At the conclusion of the two week period, but before the start of the three different methods, a timed typing test is given. Then a ten week training period in the three different methods begins. At the end of the twelve week period, a post-test is given. Results are found in Table 11.1.

TABLE 11.1

HYPOTHETICAL DATA FOR PRE AND POST-TESTS WITH BEGINNING TYPEWRITING

Group 1		Group 2		Group 3	
Pre-test	Post-test	Pre-test	Post-test	Pre-test	Post-test
12	35	29	38	17	27
17	27	12	25	22	35
13	32	17	36	10	19
10	29	22	35	8	17
8	27	15	31	13	32

To begin an analysis of covariance*, a full model should be defined. A full model is essentially a model that contains all the information relevant to the data analysis. For this specific situation, the full model is:

$$Y = b_0 + b_1X_1 + b_2X_2 + b_3X_3 + e_1, \qquad (11.1)$$

where

Y = the post-test score,

X_1 = the pre-test score,

X_2 = 1 if the score is from a member of group 1; 0 otherwise,

X_3 = 1 if the score is from a member of group 2; 0 otherwise,

b_0 = the Y-intercept,

b_1 - b_3 = the regression coefficients for X_1 - X_3, and

e_1 = the error in prediction with the full model.

If this model is solved using a multiple linear regression routine, part of the output will include the multiple correlation coefficient (R). For the present usage, since a full model is being used, the R value found from the use of equation 11.1 is labeled R_{FM}.

*Some readers who are familiar with other sources in statistics will find it hard to believe that the present approach and the approach they have previously learned give identical results. They likely remember a mass of "formulas" that they solved endlessly until the result finally arrived; or, perhaps they were allowed to use a stock analysis of covariance computer program, that through the magic of the technological age, saves the individual both the drudgery of computations, and, unfortunately in some cases, the necessity to understand the concept involved with an analysis of covariance.

Similarly, a restricted model can be developed, using the pre-test as the predictor variable:

$$Y = b_0 + b_1 X_1 + e_2, \qquad (11.2)$$

where

Y = the post-test score,

X_1 = the pre-test score,

b_0 = the Y-intercept (the b_0 value for equation 11.2 will, in general, be different from the b_0 value in equation 11.1),

b_1 = the regression coefficient for X_1 (again, the b_1 value for equation 11.2 will, in general, be different from the b_1 value found in equation 11.1),

and

e_2 = the error in prediction with the restricted model.

The restricted model will also yield an R value, and it can be labeled R_{RM}. The F test for the analysis of covariance is given by:

$$F = \frac{(R^2_{FM} - R^2_{RM})/2}{(1 - R^2_{FM})/N - 4} \ . \qquad (11.3)$$

This F test is specific for this situation. A more general F test is given by:

$$F = \frac{(R^2_{FM} - R^2_{RM})/(k - 1)}{(1 - R^2_{FM})/(N - C - k)} \ , \qquad (11.4)$$

where

k is the number of groups,
N is the number of subjects, and
C is the number of covariates.

Using the full model, an R_{FM} value of .78714 is found. Then, R^2_{FM} = .61959. For the restricted model, R_{RM} = .68903, so that R^2_{RM} = .47476.

Using equation 11.4,

$$F = \frac{(.61959 - .47476)/2}{(1 - .61959)/11} = \frac{.07241}{.03458} = 2.09.$$

This F value can be interpreted in the usual way using the F table with degrees of freedom equal to 2 and 11. The hypothesis tested in the analysis of covariance is a hypothesis that the adjusted means are equal. Multiple comparisons might also be of interest in the analysis of variance situation. Thus, it is necessary to have the adjusted (adjusted by the pre-test, or covariate) means. The adjusted means for the kth group can be found by

$$\overline{Y}_k(\text{adj}) = \overline{Y}_k - b(\overline{X}_k - \overline{X}_T), \qquad (11.5)$$

where

$\overline{Y}_k(\text{adj})$ = the adjusted criterion mean of the kth group,

$\overline{Y}_k$ = the criterion mean of the kth group,

b = the regression coefficient for the covariate (or pre-test) in the full model,

$\overline{X}_k$ = the mean of the kth group on the covariate (or pre-test), and

$\overline{X}_T$ = the overall mean on the covariate (or pre-test).

For the present data, $\overline{Y}_1 = 30$, $\overline{Y}_2 = 33$, $\overline{Y}_3 = 26$, $\overline{X}_1 = 12$, $\overline{X}_2 = 19$, $\overline{X}_3 = 14$, and $\overline{X}_T = 15$. Also, $b = .7600$. (This value is found directly from the printout for the full model). Thus, the adjusted mean for $\overline{Y}_1$, is

$$\overline{Y}_1(\text{adj}) = 30 - .7600\ (12 - 15),$$

$$\overline{Y}_1(\text{adj}) = 32.28.$$

In a similar manner, $\overline{Y}_2(\text{adj}) = 29.96$, and $\overline{Y}_3(\text{adj}) = 26.76$. Also, the adjusted SS_w term can be found directly from the printout of the full model and is equal to 199.84. The adjusted sum of squares total $SS_T(\text{adj}) = SS_T(1 - r^2)$, where r is the correlation between Y and the covariate, which in the present case is $r = .68903$, and $r^2 = .52524$. With $SS_T = 525.33$, $SS_T(\text{adj}) = (525.33)(.52524) = 275.92$.

Alternatively, it can be seen that the sum of squares for deviation from regression for the restricted model is identically equal to 275.95. The $SS_A(\text{adj})$ can be found as a residual:

$$SS_A(\text{adj}) = SS_T(\text{adj}) - SS_w(\text{adj}). \qquad (11.6)$$

For the present data, $SS_A(adj) = 275.92 - 199.84 = 76.08$.

A summary table could be generated for the analysis of covariance and is found in Table 11.2.

TABLE 11.2

SUMMARY TABLE FOR THE ANALYSIS OF COVARIANCE FOR THE DATA IN TABLE 11.1

Source of Variation	df	SS	MS	F
Among	2	76.08	38.04	2.09
Within	11	199.84	18.17	
Total	13	275.92		

The F value found in Table 11.2 is the same as the F value previously reported.

Some discussion of the analysis of covariance is necessary. As presented here, the analysis of covariance can be seen to be a test of the significance for the unique contribution of the group membership variables to the prediction of the Y variable in the presence of the covariate. The unique contribution was actually found in calculating the F test, and is equal to $R^2_{FM} - R^2_{RM}$.

While it has not been previously mentioned, the assumptions that underlie the analysis of covariance are many. They are:

1. The subjects were either randomly chosen from the same population, or were selected from the same population on the basis of the covariate measure only.
2. The covariate is unaffected by the treatments.
3. The regression of Y on the covariate is the same for all treatment populations.
4. The regression of Y on the covariate is linear.
5. The distribution of adjusted scores (an adjusted score could have been found for each Y score in the same manner as an adjusted mean was found) is normal.
6. The distribution of the adjusted scores have the same variance.

Satisfying these assumptions is somewhat more difficult than in the analysis of variance situation, if for no other reason, there are simply more assumptions. While no extensive empirical research has been specifically performed on testing the robustness of the analysis of covariance, such as has been done with the t test and the analysis of covariance, an anticipation of such research can be made. If not more than one assumption is violated, then it would seem that no great injustice is done by performing the test without any adjustments. On the other hand, it is possible to violate more assumptions simultaneously than in the simple analysis of variance situation. If the violations become marked, or if several assumptions are simultaneously violated, it would seem the technique might become relatively useless.

One additional concern should be mentioned with the analysis of covariance. It has often been attempted when little experimental control has been exercised; apparently, the expectation is that through the magic of the twentieth century, a statistical technique will take care of whatever is uncontrolled in the experimental setting. Several experimenters in the past have used students in intact groups in the school setting, run an experiment, but "covary" on either a pre-test, or perhaps a measure of intelligence. To legitimately use intact groups, an additional assumption has to be made; no systematic method has been used to assign students to classrooms. In effect, it is assumed that students have been randomly assigned to their classrooms. In the absence of the fulfillment of the assumption of randomization, to attempt the use of a traditional experimental design would be futile.

11.3 Testing the Homogeneity of Regression

One of the major assumptions in the analysis of covariance is that the regression on the covariate is the same in all treatment populations. This assumption has been considered satisfied by the formulations in the preceding section. However, if there is an interest in doing so, a test can be performed regarding the homogeneity of regression. To complete the test for the homogeneity of regression, equation 11.6 can be defined:

$$Y = b_0 + b_2X_2 + b_3X_3 + b_5X_5 + b_6X_6 + b_7X_7 + e_3, \qquad (11.6)$$

where

Y = the criterion score,
X_1 = the pre-test score,
X_2 = 1 if the score is from a member of Group 1; 0 otherwise,
X_3 = 1 if the socre is from a member of Group 2; 0 otherwise,
X_5 = the product $X_1 \cdot X_2$,
X_6 = the product $X_1 \cdot X_3$,
$X_7 = X_1 \cdot X_4$ (where X_4 = 1 if the score is from a member of Group 3; 0 otherwise),

$b_0, b_2, b_3, b_5, b_6, b_7$ = regression coefficients for the corresponding predictor variables such that the b values are specific to this equation, and

e_3 = the error in prediction with this model.

Using this model, $R^2 = .71825$. The test for homogeneity of regression can be accomplished by the use of equation 11.4 with the R^2 found from equation 11.6 as the R^2_{FM} and the R^2 found from equation 11.1 being the restricted model:

$$F = \frac{(.71825 - .61959)/2}{(1 - .71825)/9} = 1.58$$

This F value is nonsignificant, making the assumption of homogeneity of regression tenable. In this circumstance, the analysis given earlier is followed.

11.4 The Analysis of Covariance with More than One Covariate

Using a linear model approach, more than one variable can be considered with no difficulty. The post-test data in Table 11.1 are used again; two covariates are considered, an intelligence test score, and a measure of manual dexterity. Table 11.3 contains the information for this analysis.

TABLE 11.3

ANALYSIS OF COVARIANCE WITH TWO COVARIATES

Post-Test	Intelligence Score	Manual Dexterity	Group 1 = 1 0 otherwise	Group 2 = 2 0 otherwise
35	120	38	1	0
27	98	28	1	0
32	102	32	1	0
29	106	22	1	0
27	94	30	1	0
38	123	43	0	1
25	96	31	0	1
36	108	46	0	1
35	115	40	0	1
31	128	35	0	1
27	90	27	0	0
35	110	31	0	0
19	94	25	0	0
17	95	24	0	0
32	116	33	0	0

Table 11.3 is constructed so that it might be easily transformed to punch cards, and then a multiple regression can be performed. The group identifiers are found in columns 4 and 5. The group 1 identifier is given by a 1 in column 4, and the group 2 identifier is given by a 1 in column 4. A member of group 3 can be identified by having a 0 in both columns 4 and 5.

As was the case with the analysis of covariance with one covariate, a full and restricted model can be defined. The full model for the present situation is:

$$Y = b_0 + b_1X_1 + b_2X_2 + b_3X_3 + b_4X_4 + e_4, \qquad (11.7)$$

where

Y = the post-test score,

X_1 = the intelligence test score,

X_2 = the manual dexterity score,

X_3 = 1 if the score is from a member in group 1; 0 otherwise,

X_4 = 1 if the score is from a member in group 2; 0 otherwise,

b_0 = the Y-intercept,

$b_1 - b_4$ = the regression coefficient for $X_1 - X_4$, and

e_4 = the error in prediction with the full model.

A restricted model can be developed, using only the covariates as predictor variables:

$$Y = b_0 + b_1X_1 + b_2X_2 + e_5, \qquad (11.8)$$

where

Y = the post-test score,

X_1 = the intelligence test score,

X_2 = the manual dexterity score,

b_0 = the Y-intercept (this b_0 value will, in general, be different from the b_0 value from equation 11.7),

$b_1 - b_2$ = the regression coefficients for X_1 and X_2 (these regression coefficients will, in general, be different from the b_1 and b_2 values in equation 11.7), and

e_5 = the error in prediction with the restricted model.

Using the full model, an R_{FM} value of .88201 is found. Then, R^2_{FM} = .77478. For the restricted model, R_{RM} = .83961, so that R^2_{RM} = .70495.

Using equation 11.4,

$$F = \frac{(.77478 - .70495)/2}{(1 - .77478)/(15-3-2)} = 1.55.$$

This F value can be interpreted in the usual way with degrees of freedom equal to 2 and 10. For two covariates, the adjusted mean can be found for each group using equation 11.9:

$$\overline{Y}_k(\text{adj}) = \overline{Y}_k - b_1(\overline{X}_{1k} - \overline{X}_{1T}) - b_2(\overline{X}_{2k} - \overline{X}_{2T}), \qquad (11.9)$$

where

$\overline{Y}_k(\text{adj})$ = the adjusted criterion mean of the kth group,

$\overline{Y}_k$ = the criterion mean of the kth group,

b_1 = the regression coefficient for the first covariate in the full model,

$\overline{X}_{1k}$ = the mean of the kth group on the first covariate,

$\overline{X}_{1T}$ = the overall mean on the first covariate,

b_2 = the regression coefficient for the second covariate in the full model,

$\overline{X}_{2k}$ = the mean of the kth group on the second covariate, and

$\overline{X}_{2T}$ = the overall mean of the second covariate.

Additional covariates can be added with no difficulty in an analogous manner. For the present data, $\overline{Y}_1$ = 30, $\overline{Y}_2$ = 33, $\overline{Y}_3$ = 26, $\overline{X}_{11}$ = 104, $\overline{X}_{12}$ = 114, $\overline{X}_{13}$ = 101, $\overline{X}_{1T}$ = 106.33, $\overline{X}_{21}$ = 30, $\overline{X}_{22}$ = 39, $\overline{X}_{23}$ = 28, and $\overline{X}_{2T}$ = 32.33.

Also, b_1 = .19514 and b_2 = .63027 (these values are found directly from the printout for the full model).

$$\bar{Y}_1(adj) = 30 - (.19514)\left[104 - 106.33\right] - (.63027)\left[30 - 32.33\right] = 31.92.$$

$$\bar{Y}_2(adj) = 33 - (.19514)\left[114 - 106.33\right] - (.63027)\left[39 - 32.33\right] = 27.30.$$

$$\bar{Y}_3(adj) = 26 - (.19514)\left[101 - 106.33\right] - (.63027)\left[28 - 32.33\right] = 29.77.$$

The process of adjusting the means can be seen as a way to "control" to some extent the differences on the covariates. To form a summary table for the analysis of covariance with more than two covariates, the procedure is quite similar to the process described earlier for a single covariate.

The sum of squares within is found directly from the printout from the full model and is 118.32. The adjusted sum of squares total is given by $SS_T(adj) = SS_T\ (1 - R^2)$ where R is the multiple correlation between Y and the covariates, which in the present case is R = .83961 and R^2 = .70495. With SS_T = 525.33, $SS_T(adj)$ = 525.33 (1 - .70495) = 155.00. This value is also available as the sum of squares for deviation from regression for the restricted model. The adjusted sum of squares among can be found as a residual and is 155.00 - 118.32 = 36.68. The summary table is given in Table 11.4.

TABLE 11.4

SUMMARY TABLE FOR THE ANALYSIS OF COVARIANCE WITH TWO COVARIATES

Source of Variation	df	SS	MS	F
Among	2	36.68	18.34	1.55
Within	10	118.32	11.83	
Total	12	155.00		

Any reasonable number of covariates can be employed in an analysis of covariance. Potential researchers should be cautioned against using the "slop bucket" approach to using a large number of covariates simply because it is possible. Besides being non-scientific, the use of each covariate does entail the loss of one degree of freedom in the adjusted sum of squares within. Thus, a person could use 25 covariates with ease; he should be familiar enough with the data to make a reasonable interpretation of that data after the adjustments, however. A program is available (Williams and Lindem, 1972) that will automatically print-out summary tables for the analysis of variance for the criterion scores and an analysis of covariance with several covariates (up to 10). The adjusted means are also included.

11.5 Summary

The analysis of covariance has been presented in a regression formulation. The efficiency of the regression approach, when compared to a more traditional analysis, is that two linear models need to be defined, rather than solve a considerable number of related equations. Further, multiple covariates can be considered in an analogous manner to the use of a single covariate. Using four covariates is no more difficult, either conceptually or computationally, than using a single covariate in a regression approach. The use of as many as four covariates, using a conventional approach, would seem to be so complex that even advanced texts in a traditional framework would skirt the problem.

Briefly, to complete an analysis of covariance in a regression approach requires first a full model, which includes as predictor variables the covariates and the group membership variables. The restricted model would include only the covariates. An F test would then be formed from the multiple correlations from the use of the two models:

$$F = \frac{(R^2_{FM} - R^2_{RM})/(k - 1)}{(1 - R^2_{FM})/(N - C - k)}, \qquad (11.4)$$

where k is the number of groups, N is the number of subjects and C is the number of covariates.

EXERCISES

11.1 Maresh (1971) was investigating the effects of two different modes of the teaching of reading with students who would be classed as being in the sixth grade. One group of students were in a typical graded classroom; a second group of students had their reading instruction in a homogeneous (ungraded) situation (The experiment actually involved all students, grades 1-6. The focus in the present problem is at grade 6). A pre-test was given at the beginning of the school year, with post-tests given at the end of the school year. The test used was the <u>California Reading Test</u>. The subtest reported here is the Vocabulary subtest. Scores are in grade equivalents. The data follow.

Graded Group		Non-graded Group	
Pre-test	Post-test	Pre-test	Post-test
7.3	7.9	4.9	5.8
7.0	8.0	5.7	5.4
6.9	6.9	6.8	6.9
5.5	6.9	6.4	8.5
5.7	7.0	6.4	7.3
6.6	6.8	7.3	8.5
7.7	8.5	6.4	7.5
7.3	7.5	6.4	6.8
7.5	7.7	6.9	7.1
5.5	5.8		
7.0	7.5		
5.5	5.8		
5.9	7.0		
6.2	6.4		
5.1	5.7		
6.8	7.3		
5.7	7.3		
7.3	7.8		
6.6	8.0		

Perform an analysis of covariance and find the adjusted means.

11.2 Reconsider the data in Tables 11.1 and 11.3. Using three covariates, the pre-test, the intelligence test scores and the manual dexterity scores, perform an analysis of covariance on the post-test scores. Also form a summary table, and find the adjusted means for each group.

11.3 Run a test for homogeneity of regression for the data in Table 11.3. To accomplish this test, a new full model needs to be specified:

$$Y = b_0 + b_1X_3 + b_2X_4 + b_3X_6 + b_4X_7 + b_5X_8 + b_6X_9 + b_7X_{10} +$$

$$b_8X_{11} + e_6, \qquad (11.10)$$

where

Y = the post-test score,

X_1 = the intelligence test score,

X_2 = the manual dexterity score,

X_3 = 1 if the score is from a member in Group 1; 0 otherwise,

X_4 = 1 if the score is from a member in Group 2; 0 otherwise,

X_5 = 1 if the score is from a member in Group 3; 0 otherwise,

X_6 = the product of $X_1 \cdot X_3$,

X_7 = the product of $X_1 \cdot X_4$,

X_8 = the product of $X_1 \cdot X_5$,

X_9 = the product of $X_2 \cdot X_3$,

X_{10} = the product of $X_2 \cdot X_4$,

X_{11} = the product of $X_2 \cdot X_5$,

$b_0 - b_8$ = the regression coefficients for the corresponding predictor variables such that the b values are specific to this equation,

and

e_6 = the error in prediction with this model.

The model in equation 11.10 can be tested against the model in equation 11.7, using equation 11.4.

CHAPTER TWELVE

RESIDUAL GAIN ANALYSIS AND PART AND PARTIAL CORRELATION

12.1 Introduction

A technique similar to the analysis of covariance, but focusing on the residual values from regressing the post-test on the pre-test, is the residual gain analysis. Unfortunately, because the two techniques are similar, and because statistical authors have been a bit sloppy in writing about the analysis of covariance and the residual gain analysis, several applied researchers have concluded that they are in fact equivalent techniques. Jennings (1972) contrasted the linear models for the two approaches, and Williams and Buzahora (1973) gave extensive empirical comparisons between the two approaches.

Closely related to the residual gain analysis is a correlational technique called part correlation. Finally, partial correlation has been used whenever the effect of a given variable is to be completely removed from an analysis.

12.2 The Residual Gain Analysis

DuBois (1957, 1970) has worked extensively with the residual gain analysis. Essentially, the residual gain analysis is an analysis of variance performed on the residuals on the post-test data when using the pre-test as the predictor. So that the residual gain analysis and the analysis of covariance can be contrasted, the data in Table 11.1 are analyzed using the residual gain analysis. As a model, this analysis can be accomplished in two stages with an ordinary multiple regression program. The first model is:

$$Y = b_0 + b_1 X_1 + e_1, \qquad (12.1)$$

where

Y = the post-test score,

X_1 = the pre-test score,

b_0 = the Y-intercept,

b_1 = the regression coefficient for X_1, and

e_1 = the error in prediction for this model.

It can be recalled that equation 12.1 is identically the same model as the restricted model (equation 11.2) for the analysis of covariance. The focus in the residual gain analysis is on the residual errors (e_1) for each subject. These residual errors become the criterion scores, and the group membership variable(s) are used to complete the residual gain analysis. The model is as follows for the data in Table 11.1:

$$Y' = b_0 + b_2X_2 + b_3X_3 + e_2, \qquad (12.1)$$

where

Y' = the residual errors found from the use of equation 12.1,

X_2 = 1 if the score is from a member of group 1; 0 otherwise,

X_3 = 1 if the score is from a member of group 2; 0 otherwise,

b_0 = the Y-intercept (and equal to the mean residual gain for group 3),

b_2 = the regression coefficient for X_2,

b_3 = the regression coefficient for X_3, and

e_2 = the error in prediction for this model.

The use of the residual gain analysis has been based upon the following considerations: the residual gain scores will be uncorrelated with initial status, whereas it can be expected that the raw gain scores will show a negative correlation with initial states; whenever all subjects do not start at a common point, the residual score nevertheless:

1. can be defined precisely and accurately,
2. the residual does not require the use of a ratio scale to measure initial and final states, and
3. is completely independent of and uncorrelated with initial status.

Table 12.1 contains the residuals found when regressing the post-test scores on the pre-test scores.

TABLE 12.1

RESIDUAL GAIN SCORES FOR THE DATA IN TABLE 11.1

Group 1	Group 2	Group 3
7.49585	-1.75830	-4.10831
-4.10831	-2.50415	0.28752
3.77502	4.89169	-7.06248
2.93752	0.28752	-7.62082
2.37918	1.33336	3.77502

The data in Table 12.1 are then subjected to the usual analysis of variance, with one modification. Because one degree of freedom is used by the pre-test, the degrees of freedom for within are 11 (the same as in the analysis of covariance) rather than 12. This This analysis is shown in Table 12.2.

TABLE 12.2

SUMMARY TABLE FOR A RESIDUAL GAIN ANALYSIS

Source of Variation	df	SS	MS	F
Among	2	75.55	37.77	2.07
Within	11	200.37	18.21	
Total	13	275.92		

Comparisons between Table 12.2 with the residual gain analysis and Table 11.2 with the analysis of covariance would suggest a close, but not identical relationship. The same SS_T is involved in both analyses. The sum of squares among and within differ only slightly in the two tables. Actually, the relationship between the two analyses can be fairly divergent.

12.3 Partial Correlation

The partial correlation between two variables is the correlation that exists between them after the effect of one or more control variables has been taken out. More specifically, the partial correlation between two variables is the correlation between the residuals of those same variables when they have been regressed on the same control variables.

Using the data from Tables 11.1 and 11.3, the question might be asked, "What is the partial correlation between the pre-test and the post-test after the effect of intelligence has been taken (partialled) out?" The approach suggested here would be to first use intelligence as a predictor of the pre-test, and then use intelligence as a predictor of the post-test. The residuals found in both regression analyses would then be correlated. The resulting correlation is a partial correlation between the pre-test and post-test. Table 12.3 contains the residuals from using intelligence as a predictor of the pre-test and using intelligence as a predictor of the post-test.

TABLE 12.3

RESIDUALS FROM USING INTELLIGENCE AS A PREDICTOR OF THE PRE-TEST AND OF USING INTELLIGENCE AS A PREDICTOR OF THE POST-TEST

Pre-Test Score	Post-Test Score	Intelligence Score	Pre-Test Residuals	Post-Test Residuals
12	35	120	-6.27185	0.23097
17	27	98	3.99504	0.44453
13	32	102	-0.96259	3.95116
10	29	106	-4.92020	-0.54221
8	27	94	-4.04735	1.93791
29	38	123	10.00995	2.11095
12	25	96	-0.52615	-0.80878
17	36	108	1.60100	5.71111
22	35	115	4.92517	2.09769
15	31	128	-5.18708	-6.75578
17	27	90	5.91026	3.43129
22	35	110	6.12219	3.96442
10	19	94	-2.04735	-6.06209
8	17	95	-4.28676	-8.43542
13	32	116	-4.31422	-1.27565

If a correlation is performed with the residuals in the usual manner, the correlation is .56. If the pre-test is called X_1, the post-test is Y, and the intelligence score is X_2, then the partial correlation is usually notated $r_{1Y.2}$. This notation indicates that variable 2 (intelligence) has been partialled out of both variable 1 and the Y variable. It is of course possible to partial out more than one variable. It is only necessary to run the control variables as predictors of the two or more variables on which the partial correlation is to be found. The residuals could then be correlated in a like manner as was done in the present situation.

When the student consults other texts on partial correlation, he will likely see either some complex equations for solving for the partial correlations, or an elaborate matrix solution is presented. It is felt that by presenting partial correlations directly as the correlation between two sets of residuals has more intuitive appeal than other approaches.* Computationally, partial correlations can be generated from a computer in a host of different ways. For the researcher, an understanding would seem to be more important than the details of computation.

12.4 Part Correlation

The concept of part correlation is very similar to partial correlation. In part correlation, one variable is modified by regressing that variable on a control variable and the residuals are found. These residuals are then correlated with another unmodified variable. Because the control variable is used with only "part" of the variables to be correlated (the modified variable), the name part correlation is given. For example, there might be an interest in finding the part correlation between the pre-test modified by the intelligence test scores (that is, "take-out" the effect of intelligence in the pre-test scores) and the post-test scores (unmodified). To solve for this part correlation, the correlation can be found directly for the scores in column 2 and column 4 in Table 12.3. The part correlation is .38. The notation for correlating a modified variable (the pre-test, of X_1) which has been modified by a control variable (the intelligence test score, or X_2) with a third variable (the post-test, or Y) is $r_{(1.2)Y}$.

It should be pointed out that a multiple part correlation has already been made in this chapter, although no mention was made at the time. When the residual gain scores were analyzed by the analysis of variance by using a linear model, the Y scores were modified by the pre-test scores. A multiple regression was then run between the residual gains and the two membership variables. This process yields a multiple correlation that, because the criterion scores are modified (and are in fact, residuals), the resulting multiple correlation was actually a multiple part correlation. A much more extensive coverage on part, partial, multiple part and multiple partial correlation can be found in DuBois (1957).

*Other texts give equations for solving for partial correlations directly from the original correlations. To find $r_{1Y.2}$, the following equation can be solved:

$$r_{1Y.2} = \frac{r_{1Y} - r_{12}r_{Y2}}{\sqrt{(1 - r_{12}^2)(1 - r_{Y2}^2)}} .$$

12.5 Summary

Three related concepts have been presented in this chapter. The residual gain analysis is a technique for measuring change from a pre-test and post-test wherein the post-test scores are regressed upon the pre-test scores, and the resulting residuals are then analyzed by the usual analysis of variance technique, after modifying the degrees of freedom for within by subtracting one.

If a variable (or set of variables) are used as predictors separately for two variables X and Y, then the correlation of the residuals from these regressions would be called a partial correlation.

If a variable (or set of variables) is used as predictors for the X variable, and the residuals are correlated with an unmodified Y variable this would be called a part correlation.

EXERCISES

12.1 Perform a residual gain analysis on the data in problem 11.1.

12.2 For the data in Table 11.3, find the residuals from regressing the pre-test (X_1) and the post-test (Y) separately on the intelligence test scores (X_2) and the manual dexterity scores (X_3). Then correlate the resulting residuals. The notation for this partial correlation would be $r_{1Y.23}$.

12.3 For the data in Table 11.3, find the residuals from regressing the pre-test (X_1) on the manual dexterity scores (X_3) and the post-test on the manual dexterity scores. The resulting correlation is a partial correlation and is denoted $r_{1Y.3}$.

12.4 For the data in Table 11.3, find the part correlation between manual dexterity (as an unmodified variable) and the pre-test score, partialling out the intelligence score.

12.5 Bleeker and Kelly (1971) were interested in finding whether there was a correlation between the Mental Age scores on twenty subjects on two diagnostic tests, the Illinois Test of Psycholinguistic Abilities (ITPA) and the Peabody Picture Vocabulary Test (PPVT).

The subjects chosen were children ranging in age from 5 years 9 months to 17 years, who had come to an evaluation center for exceptional children for appraisal.

DATA

Subjects	X_1 Chronological Age (months)	X_2 ITPA Mental Age (months)	X_3 Peabody Mental Age (months)
1	69	45	52
2	162	114	193
3	144	123	216
4	109	92	82
5	118	98	124
6	204	84	120
7	121	120	148
8	103	65	94
9	139	91	112
10	189	90	124
11	165	37	41
12	166	104	130
13	159	121	156
14	139	61	42
15	84	81	77
16	187	79	84
17	89	74	73
18	94	92	102
19	82	69	61
20	163	102	139

They found a correlation of .90 between the ITPA and PPVT. However, it would seem that some of this correlation was due to chronological age. Find the partial correlation between the ITPA and PPVT, partialling out chronological age. The resulting partial correlation must be interpreted in the light that a very specific population is being tested; children referred to a state agency for evaluation might be inferred to differ from a normal population in the areas being tested.

CHAPTER THIRTEEN

THE MEASUREMENT OF TRENDS

13.1 Introduction

Quite often in educational research, the researcher is able to obtain measurements taken at different time intervals. While there are a considerable variety of ways that trends can be manipulated in the educational setting, two kinds of problems are of specific interest. First, several separate groups can be considered where the different groups have been involved in an instructional unit for varying lengths of time. The second situation occurs when two or more groups are measured several times over an extended period of time.

13.2 Several Groups with Varying Amounts of Instruction

Suppose five groups of students are given varying amounts of practice in learning to type. The five groups are given the following amounts of practice: Group 1, 15 hours of instruction; Group 2, 30 hours of instruction; Group 3, 45 hours of instruction; Group 4, 60 hours of instruction; and Group 5, 75 hours of instruction. In addition to differences among the groups, the trend of the data over the varying instructional periods is also of interest. Table 13.1 contains the scores for the five groups.

TABLE 13.1

FIVE GROUPS OF STUDENTS WITH VARYING AMOUNTS OF INSTRUCTIONAL PERIODS OF TYPING WITH NUMBER OF WORDS TYPED PER MINUTE (ARTIFICIAL DATA)

Group 1	Group 2	Group 3	Group 4	Group 5
26	39	46	48	50
24	37	41	43	45
23	34	38	37	42
23	31	37	32	40
20	29	34	31	35
16	28	32	31	28

First, it is useful to run an ordinary analysis of variance. The summary table for the data in Table 13.1 are shown in Table 13.2.

TABLE 13.2

SUMMARY TABLE FOR FIVE GROUPS OF STUDENTS WITH VARYING AMOUNTS OF INSTRUCTIONAL PERIODS OF TYPING WITH NUMBER OF WORDS TYPED PER MINUTE

Source of Variation	df	SS	MS	F
Among	4	1236.00	309.00	9.22
Within	25	838.00	33.52	
Total	29	2074.00		

The significant F value, in addition to showing differences among the means of the groups, also would allow for the possibility of a trend; it does not guarantee a trend. The search for a trend can be made through the use of polynomial regression.

13.3 Polynomial Regression

A polynomial is a mathematical function that represents a criterion variable (Y) in an equation that contains the X variable represented with several integral powers. More specifically, a polynomial equation is of the form

$$Y = b_0 + b_1 X + b_2 X^2 + b_3 X^3 + b_4 X^4 + \ldots + b_k X^k . \qquad (13.1)$$

When k = 1, equation 13.1 becomes

$Y = b_0 + b_1 X$; this is the equation of a straight line. When k = 2, equation 13.1 becomes

$Y = b_0 + b_1 X + b_2 X^2$, a second degree equation (sometimes called a quadratic equation).

When k = 3, equation 13.1 becomes

$Y = b_0 + b_1 X + b_2 X^2 + b_3 X^3$, a third degree equation. In a like manner, a polynomial equation of any degree can be formed. In general, the highest degree polynomial that can be found will be of one less degree than the number of distinct points on the predictor variable. If there are five distinct points, then the highest degree polynomial equation would be the fourth degree polynomial ($Y = b_0 + b_1 X + b_2 X^2 + b_3 X^3 + b_4 X^4$).

13.4 The Use of Polynomial Regression to Find a Trend

When the data are in equally distant intervals such as is true for the data in Table 13.1, a useful transformation of the data can be made. If 15 hours of instruction are made equal to one unit of instruction, then Group 1 has had one unit of instruction, Group 2 has had two units of instruction, Group 3 has had three units of instruction, Group 4 has had four units of instruction, and Group 5 has had five units of instruction. Thus, the five groups represent five distinct points; the highest degree polynomial that could be found using this data would be a fourth degree polynomial. Table 13.3 contains the data from Table 13.1 except that the subjects in Group 1, with hours of instruction are shown as having 1 unit (15 hours) of instruction. Similarly, Group 2 subjects are shown with 2 units of instruction etc., through the Group 5 subjects, who are shown with five units of instruction. The squares, cubes (third power), and fourth power are also included.

TABLE 13.3

DATA FROM TABLE 13.1 WITH SQUARES, CUBES, THIRD AND FOURTH POWER SHOWN

Y	X	X^2	X^3	X^4
26	1	1	1	1
24	1	1	1	1
23	1	1	1	1
23	1	1	1	1
20	1	1	1	1
16	1	1	1	1
39	2	4	8	16
37	2	4	8	16
34	2	4	8	16
31	2	4	8	16
29	2	4	8	16
28	2	4	8	16
46	3	9	27	81
41	3	9	27	81
38	3	9	27	81
37	3	9	27	81
34	3	9	27	81
32	3	9	27	81
48	4	16	64	256
43	4	16	64	256
37	4	16	64	256
32	4	16	64	256
31	4	16	64	256
31	4	16	64	256
50	5	25	125	625
45	5	25	125	625
42	5	25	125	625
40	5	25	125	625
35	5	25	125	625
28	5	25	125	625

In performing a polynomial regression, it is helpful to begin with the simplest equation, that is, one of the form $Y = b_0 + b_1X$, the equation of a straight line. If a least squares solution is performed, the equation Y = 22 + 4X is found. This equation is fit to the data of Table 13.3 in Figure 13.1.

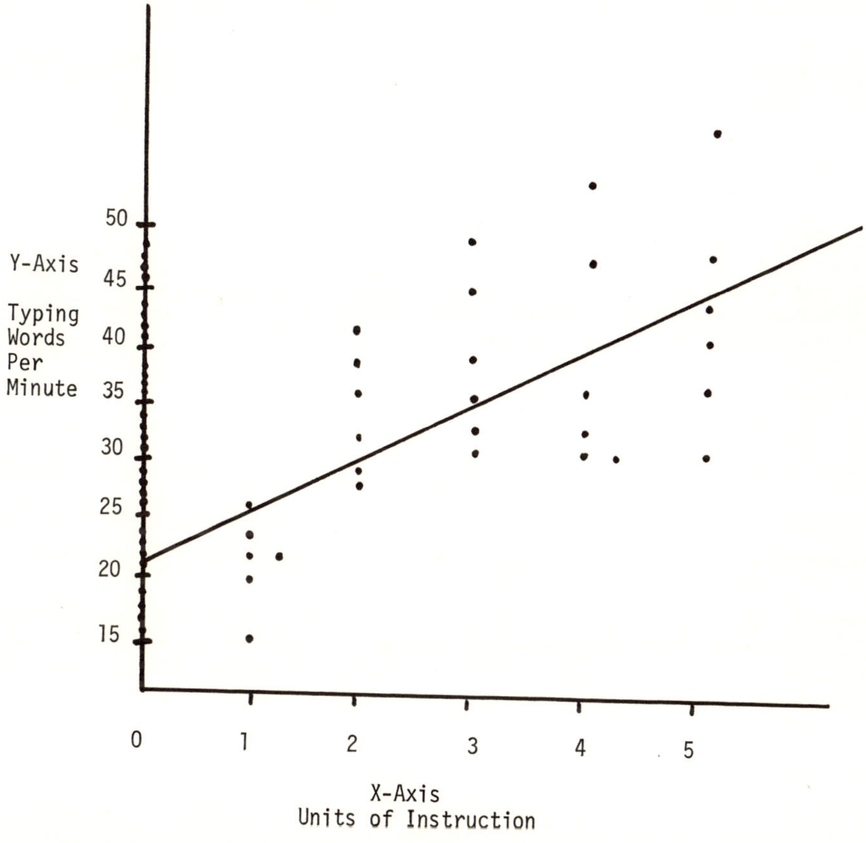

Figure 13.1 Graph of First Degree Equation for the Data in Table 13.3 (Y = 22 + 4X).

Also, an analysis of variance for the regression could be found for the equation, $Y = 22 + 4X$. The interest can be directed to the sum of squares due to linear regression (SS_{LINEAR}). For the first degree polynomial, $SS_{LINEAR} = 960.00$. In that the sum of squares due to differences among groups is $SS_A = 1236.0$ (from Table 13.2), and SS_{LINEAR} is 960.0, it can be seen that most of the differences among groups is attributable to the linear trend; if the difference $SS_A - SS_{LINEAR} = 1236.0 - 960.0 = 276.0$ is found, the value 276.0 is the amount of deviation from a linear trend.

13.5 Polynomial Regression with a Second Degree Equation

A second degree polynomial is of the form $Y = b_0 + b_1X + b_2X^2$. There are two general kinds of second degree curves; one second degree curve rises until it reaches a maximum, and then recedes. A second form of the second degree curve goes down until it reaches a minimum, and then starts back up. While the details of second degree polynomials are found in any textbook on analytic geometry, it is instructive to inspect graphs of the two second degree polynomials. See Figures 13.2 and 13.3.

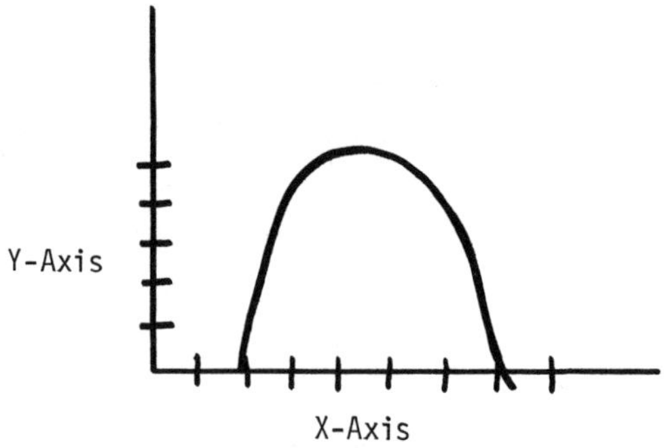

Figure 13.2 A second degree polynomial that reaches a maximum and then recedes.

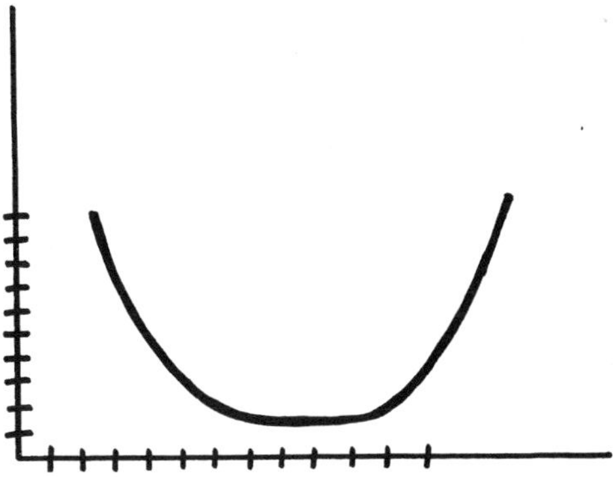

Figure 13.3 A second degree polynomial that reaches a minimum and then goes up.

The importance of a second degree polynomial is that it might be a better description of a research situation than a linear (or straight line) relationship. For example, it has been hypothesized, and to some degree shown, that measures of anxiety plotted against achievement would show a second degree curve relationship. That is, low anxious and high anxious students do not perform as well as students who represent a moderate degree of anxiety. Thus, performance is maximized in the middle scores, and Figure 13.2 might represent the relationship between achievement and anxiety fairly well.

On the other hand, the present interest is to force the data in Table 13.3 to fit a second degree polynomial, by means of the least squares procedure; this process can be performed with a computer using the regression program. The resulting equation is $Y = 11 + 13.43X - 1.57X^2$. The sum of squares attributable to regression for the second degree equation is 1167.41. Previously, it was found with the first degree equation that the sum of squares accounted for by linear regression was 960. Thus, 1167.41 - 960 = 207.41 are the sum of squares uniquely attributable to the second degree polynomial. In a manner similar to the linear trend, the deviation from a second degree trend can be found. If the value 1167.41 is subtracted from the SS_A term, 1236.0, the resulting value, 68.59, is the sum of squares for deviation from a second degree trend. The second degree polynomial for the data in Table 13.3 is shown in Figure 13.4.

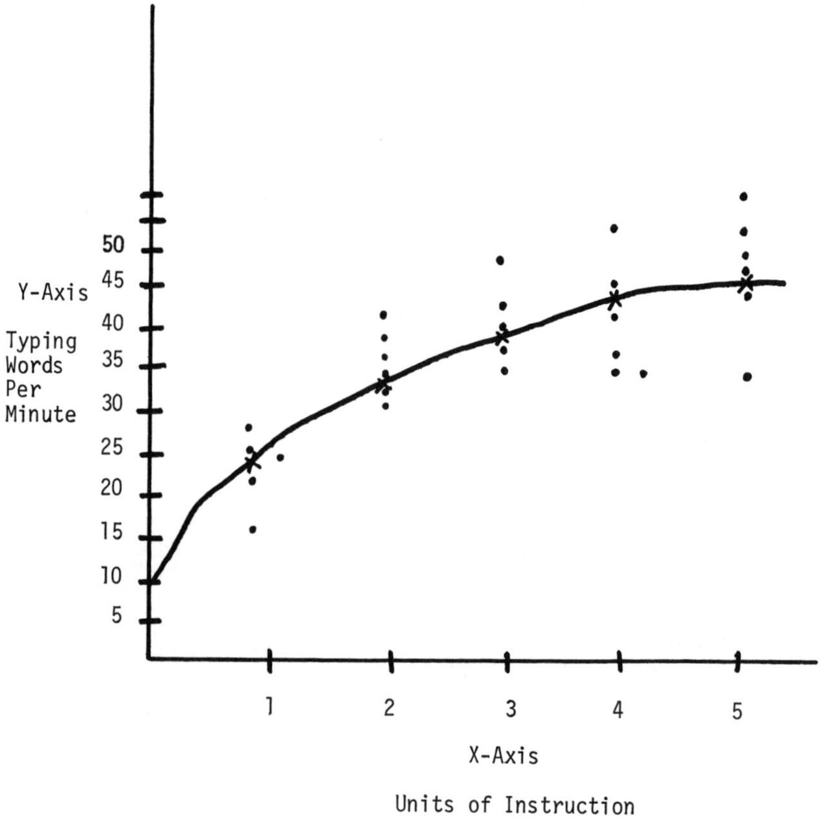

Figure 13.4 Graph of a Second Degree Equation for the Data in Table 13.3
$$(Y = 11 + 13.43X - 1.57X^2).$$

13.6 Polynomial Regression for a Third Degree Equation

In a similar manner, the data in Table 13.3 could be forced into a third degree equation. A third degree equation is of the form $Y = b_0 + b_1X + b_2X^2 + b_3X^3$, and there are two general kinds of graphs that can be formed. One graph occurs when the graph is going up, then turns down, and then turns up again. A second graph occurs when the graph is going down, then goes up, and then goes down again. Figures 13.5 and 13.6 show these types of graphs.

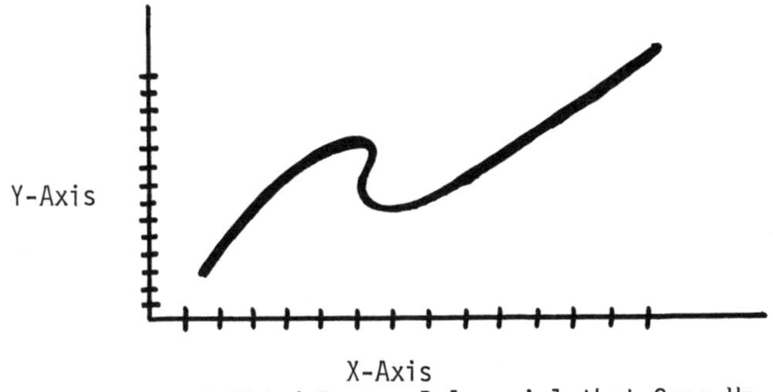

Figure 13.5 A Third Degree Polynomial that Goes Up, Then Down, and Up Again.

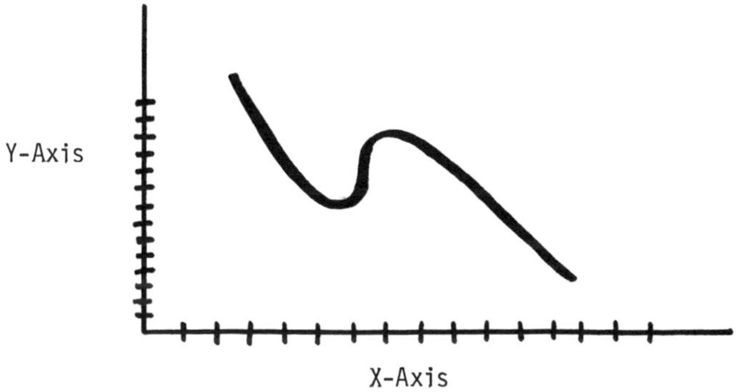

Figure 13.6 A Third Degree Polynomial that Goes Down, Then Up, then Down Again.

In fitting the data from Table 13.3 to a third degree equation, the following equation results:

$$Y = -3.02 + 33.13X - 9.08X^2 + .83X^3.$$

Also, the third degree equation accounts for 1226.58 sum of squares; in that a second degree equation accounted for a sum of squares total equal to 1167.41, the third degree equation uniquely accounts for 1226.58 - 1167.41 = 59.17. Also, the deviation from a third degree trend is 1236 - 1226.58 = 9.42. This value is used later in the summary table as the deviation from regression. The graph for fitting the data in Table 13.3 is shown in Figure 13.7.

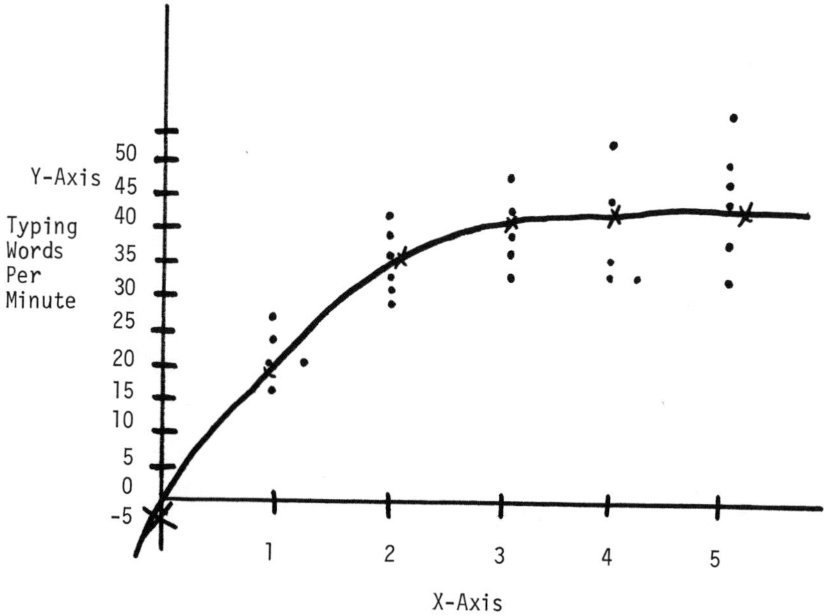

Figure 13.7 Graph of a Third Degree Equation for the Data in Table 13.3
$(Y = -3.02 + 33.13X - 9.08X^2 + .83X^3)$

Before going on to a fourth degree polynomial, a comment would be useful in regard to the three graphs of the data for Table 13.3. On the one hand, the curves are fairly similar to one another. This is due to much of the accounted variability being due to the linear trend. While Figures 13.4 and 13.7 are not straight lines, neither do they look much like second or third degree trends. If Figure 13.7 is used to describe the data, it might be conjectured that the data are represented by a curve that seems to have a rapid acceleration at first, but later on, only a moderate increase. The student who is either familiar with the research on learning, or familiar with logarithmic functions, would likely try to fit a logarithmic curve to the data. The logarithm could be found for each value of X, and then a regression program could be run with the equation $Y = b_0 + b_1 \log X$. (See exercise 13.1).

A second point is necessary in regard to another idea in regard to a polynomial of a given degree. When an equation is of the first degree, it does not change direction. When an equation is of third degree, the graph will change directions twice. In general, an equation of degree k will change directions k - 1 times.* Thus odd degree polynomials (that is, of degree 1, 3, 5, etc.) will have in common the feature that they end going the same direction that they started. An equation of an even degree (2, 4, 6, etc.) ends going the opposite direction from which it started.

13.7 Polynomial Regression with Fourth Degree and Higher Degrees of Polynomials

The process described for the first, second and third degree polynomials can be extended up to k - 1 where k is the number of distinct data points on the X variable. For the data in Table 13.3, there are five distinct data points, so that the fourth degree polynomial <u>can</u> be considered. This process could be extended to its ridiculous extreme; in general, the higher the degree of the polynomial, the more probable it is that the researcher will have difficulty in interpreting the data.

For the data under consideration, the sum of squares accounted for by a fourth degree polynomial is 1066.57. This is a decrease in the amount of sum of squares accounted by both a second and third degree polynomial. While there might be some novelty value associated with this decrease, it is a good indication that a third degree polynomial is as high a polynomial that needs to be considered.

13.8 A Summarization of the Fitting of Data to a Polynomial

The previous calculations in Table 13.2 and also in regard to the calculations for the first, second and third degree polynomial can be put into a summary table. The sum of squares among from Table 13.2 (equal to 1236.00) can be partitioned into four components: sum of squares due to linear regression (SS_{LINEAR}), sum of squares due to the second degree regression (SS_{SECOND}), sum of squares due to the third degree regression (SS_{THIRD}), and the deviation from regression (SS_{DEV}). From section 13.4, SS_{LINEAR} = 960.00; from section 13.5, SS_{SECOND} = 207.41; and, from section

*For those students familiar with calculus, it might be recalled that the existence of inflection points will modify this statement a bit. An inflection point occurs when the curve does not actually change directions, but at the inflection point, has a slope of 0.

13.6, SS_{THIRD} = 59.17. Then, SS_{DEV} can be found as a residual: SS_{DEV} = 1236.00 - 960.00 - 207.41 - 59.17 = 9.42. Each of these sources of variation has one degree of freedom. The SS_W term is as before in Table 13.2; SS_W = 838.00. This information can be put into a summary table; see Table 13.4.

TABLE 13.4

SUMMARY TABLE FOR THE TREND ANALYSIS OF THE DATA IN TABLE 13.2

Sources of Variation	df	SS	MS	F
Linear Regression	1	960.00	960.00	28.639
Second degree regression	1	207.41	207.41	6.187
Third degree regression	1	59.17	59.17	1.765
Deviation from regression*	1	9.42	9.42	.281
Within	25	838.00	33.52	
Total	29	2074.00		

The F values are each formed by dividing the corresponding mean square term by the mean square within term.

The process of trend analysis is remarkedly similar to the hierarchical model encountered in Chapter Nine. That is, the linear portion is measured first, and the sum of squares accounted by the first degree equation (linear equation) is found. Then a new model is used that includes a second degree component in the equation. The additional sum of squares are calculated for the second degree equation. Additional terms can be found in a similar manner. The point is that each additional higher degree equation is fitted only after all lower degree equations have been fitted. Hopefully, only a small number of components are necessary to describe the data.

13.9 A Repeated Measures Design

A researcher may have an interest in the differential effect of two or more methods of instruction over time; thus, measures can be taken at specified intervals on the several instructional methods. From the point of view of the experiment, a repeated measures design can be conceptualized as a treatments X subjects design repeated for each instructional method.**

*Had a fourth degree polynomial been included, the deviation from regression would not occur as a specific source of variation; accordingly, a rule of thumb is that a curve fitting should not go beyond the $(k - 2)^{th}$ degree.

**This design is called a Type I design by Lindquist (1953).

To make the example more specific, suppose a researcher is interested in investigating the differences among three approaches to a human relations experience.*

The three different approaches toward the human relations groups selected are (1) structured sessions in which the group participates toward concrete problem solving, (2) an unstructured group, where the group decides upon its own goals, and (3) a group designed to allow the individual to focus on his personal problems with the interest being to help solve these problems. Five groups with 7-9 individuals in each group are assigned to each of the three human relation group situations; i.e., there are five separate groups for each treatment situation. Each group is to have a two hour session once a week for four weeks.

While there are several things that might be of interest to measure, the researcher is interested specifically in the amount of aggression exhibited in the group setting.

Videotapes are made of all sessions, and a group of five experts independently judge the amount of aggression expressed during the sessions on a continuum from 0 to 10, where 0 represents no aggression and 10 represents an extreme amount of aggression. The measurements are made with the group as the unit of analysis. The score to be used is the mean of the five ratings. Results are as follows:

TABLE 13.5

GROUP SCORES FROM THREE HUMAN RELATION GROUP METHODS FOR FIVE SESSIONS (ARTIFICIAL DATA)

Method 1 (Structured Groups)

Group	Session 1	Session 2	Session 3	Session 4
1	3.2	3.4	3.2	2.8
2	4.6	4.0	3.8	3.4
3	5.0	3.8	5.0	3.2
4	2.0	2.0	2.4	1.6
5	3.6	3.2	3.4	3.0

*By human relations experience is meant the meeting of a group of people that has variously been called the T-Group (training group), the encounter group, or some similar name.

Method 2 (Unstructured Groups)

Group	Session 1	Session 2	Session 3	Session 4
6	6.2	5.8	6.8	5.0
7	3.6	3.8	7.2	5.4
8	4.0	6.8	7.8	6.0
9	5.0	5.8	6.0	5.0
10	4.8	5.0	6.4	5.8

Method 3 (Personal Problems)

Group	Session 1	Session 2	Session 3	Session 4
11	7.4	7.6	6.8	5.2
12	6.4	6.4	5.6	4.0
13	7.0	6.6	6.6	6.0
14	5.8	7.4	5.0	4.8
15	6.4	5.2	4.0	3.6

Before proceeding with an analysis, it is useful to differentiate between three terms (fixed effects, random effects, mixed effects) as they relate to experimental design.

When the experimenter purposely selects specific categories, the term fixed effects applies. The one-way, two-way, and higher n way designs are usually of this type. The idea is that the experimenter fixes the phenomena of interest. On the other hand, the categories that are used may be of no particular interest in themselves, but are interesting only insofar as they might represent some larger population; such a situation is referred to as random effects. The simplest example of this kind of design is the treatments X subjects design; typically, the subjects used in a treatments X subjects design are viewed as being a random sample rather than being of experimental interest as specified individuals. It is of course possible that both kinds of designs could be present in the same design; such a design would be called a mixed design. The data in the present design (Table 13.5) is a mixed design. To show that this is so, if the different treatments are disregarded, then the data can be viewed as a simple treatments X subjects design, where the term "treatments" refers to the various groups. If, however, the data in each cell is viewed as being unrelated to the data in other cells, then the data could be analyzed as a two-way analysis of variance. Thus, the design is said to be "mixed." One of the peculiarities of mixed designs is that they will normally contain more than one error term, so that their execution and interpretations are somewhat more complicated.

To analyze the data in Table 13.5, it is first useful to define several variables:

Y = the criterion variable,

from equation 13.3, $SS_{TREND} = 8.63$;

from equation 13.7, $SS_{ERROR_2} = 39.71$. To find the interaction, a method similar to the one used in Chapter Eight can be used. The sum of squares attributed to regression for the full model (equation 13.7) is 105.58. The sum of squares attributed to regression for equation 13.6 is 87.50. The difference between these two values is equal to the interaction. Thus, $SS_{METH\ X\ TREND} = 105.58 - 87.50 = 18.08$. A summary table that would contain the foregoing information would appear as follows:

TABLE 13.6

SUMMARY TABLE FOR THE HUMAN RELATION GROUPS DATA IN TABLE 13.5

Source of Variation	df	SS	MS	F
Among Subjects				
Method	2	78.87	39.44	18.69**
Error (a)	12	25.27	2.11	
Total Among Subjects	14	104.14		
Within Subjects				
TREND	3	8.63	2.88	7.20**
METH X TREND	6	18.08	3.01	7.52**
ERROR (b)	36	14.44	.40	
Total Within Subjects	45	41.15		
Total	59	145.29		

**Significant at .01 level

The two entries in the sum of squares column in Table 13.6 that did not have a procedure previously given for it were $SS_{ERROR(a)}$ and $SS_{ERROR(b)}$. What has occurred here is that the error ($SS_{ERROR_2} = 39.71$) from the full model for the two way portion of the analysis is split into two components, $SS_{ERROR(a)}$ and $SS_{ERROR(b)}$. $SS_{ERROR(a)}$ is equal to $SS_{SUBJECTS} - SS_{METH} = 25.27$. Then, $SS_{ERROR(b)} = SS_{ERROR_2} - SS_{ERROR(a)} = 14.44$. The $SS_{ERROR(b)}$ could have been found in another way: $SS_{ERROR(b)} = SS_{ERROR_1} - SS_{METH\ X\ TREND}$.

To interpret the data in Table 13.5, it is necessary to use the appropriate error term with a given mean square ratio. The MS_{METH} is tested by $MS_{ERROR(b)}$; the remaining sources of variation (trend, and the interaction of methods by trend) are tested by $SS_{ERROR(b)}$.

Interpreting the results of Table 13.6 is compounded by the fact that all three effects (methods, trend, and the methods X trend interaction) are significant. Thus, it would be useful to look at two additional aspects of the analysis--the trend analysis as given earlier in this chapter, and then draw a graph of the results.

Since there were four sessions, up to a second* degree polynomial could be considered in fitting the data. The first degree equation is given by:

$Y = b_0 + b_{29}X_{29} + e_7$; when this equation is used with the data in Table 13.5, $SS_{LINEAR} = 2.50$.

For a second degree polynomial, $Y = b_0 + b_{29}X_{29} + b_{30}X_{30} + e_8$; when this equation is used with the data in Table 13.5, $SS_{LINEAR + SECOND} = 7.32$. Thus, $SS_{SECOND} = 7.32 - 2.50 = 4.82$.

These results are recorded in a table very similar to Table 13.6, except that the trend effect has been split into three components (linear, second, and deviation from trend); these results are in Table 13.7.

*Using the rule of thumb in the note to Table 13.4, no curve fitting would go beyond a (k - 2) polynomial equation.

TABLE 13.7

SUMMARY TABLE WITH TREND ANALYSIS FOR THE HUMAN RELATIONS GROUP DATA IN TABLE 13.5

Source of Variation	df	SS	MS	F
Among Subjects				
Methods	2	78.87	39.44	18.69**
Error (a)	12	25.27	2.11	
Total Among Subjects	14	104.14		
Within Subjects				
Trend				
Linear regression	1	2.50	2.50	6.25*
Second degree regression	1	4.82	4.82	12.05**
Deviation from regression	1	1.31	1.31	3.28
Total Trend	3	8.63		
METH X TREND	6	18.08	3.01	7.52**
Error (b)	36	14.44	.40	
Total Within Subjects	45	41.15		
Total	59	145.29		

*Significant at .05 level
**Significant at .01 level

In interpreting the data in Table 13.7, the following points seem salient:

(1) There is a significant ($p < .01$) methods effect, indicating differences between the three human relations treatments;
(2) In regard to trend, the stronger effect appears to be the quadratic trend (significant at the .01 level), although the linear trend is also significant ($p < .05$);
(3) There is a methods X trends interaction, suggesting that the trend is different regarding the three methods.

Figure 13.8 should add additional light to the interpretation.

Mean of Levels of Aggression in each
Method at each Session

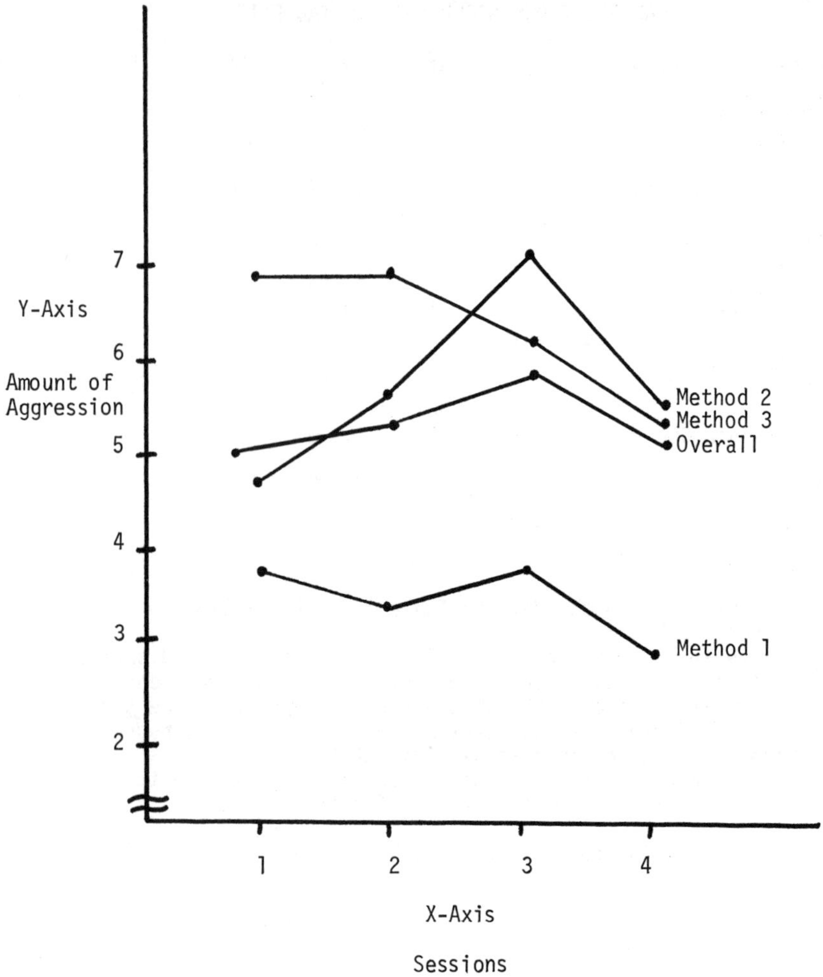

Figure 13.8 Level of Aggression for Three Human Relation Groups

The difference in trend is seen in Figure 13.8. Method 3 seems to be the most different of the three methods trends. Aggression is stable for the first two sessions, and then starts dropping off sharply. Method 1 shows some small variation for the first three sessions, with aggression dropping sharply on the last session. Method 2 shows a definite quadratic (second degree) trend. The overall trend shows a slowly increasing amount of aggression for the first three sessions, with a marked drop at the fourth session. The interaction of methods X trend is clearly demonstrated. This interaction is largely due to Method 3.

Thus, the data from this experiment might be interpreted in the following manner: The structured groups (Method 1) show less aggression at every session than the remaining methods. The unstructured groups (Method 2) show an increasing amount of aggression until the last session. The final session shows a decrease from the third session. The personal problems groups (Method 3) initially show a high amount of aggression, but the aggression starts reducing after the second session. All three types of groups show a decreasing amount of aggression for the fourth session.

13.10 A Note of Computer Accuracy

It may well be the case that if the reader has attempted all of the problems encountered on regression in this text, that on at least a few occasions, the solutions will not always agree identically to the solutions given here. Assuming that the problems have been correctly solved, two reasons will account for most of the differences found. First, there are a host of regression solutions, and the different alogarithms used may yield slightly different results. Second, as the number of variables becomes fairly large (whenever the number of variables is more than half the sample size), the estimates formed are somewhat less stable. In research applications, increasing the sample size will help allay this second problem.

13.11 Summary

Two approaches to trend analysis are given in the present chapter. One approach to measuring trend involves measuring the amount of exposure to the experimental variable and fitting succeedingly higher degree polynomials to fit the data.

The second approach includes a repeated measures design; thus, each subject is measured at specified intervals, and the effect of the trend is measured.

EXERCISES

13.1 Taking the data from Table 13.3 fit an equation of the form

$$Y = b_0 + b_1 \log_{10} X.$$

Hint: This can be accomplished with a logarithmic transformation (to the base of 10) of the X variable. Actually, whether the transformation is made to the base 10 or the base **e**, the result, in the practical sense, is the same. The two different bases will account for the same amount of variance, and therefore will produce the same correlation.

13.2 Again using the data from Table 13.3, fit an equation of the form

$$\log_{10} Y = b_0 + b_1 X.$$

13.3 A business education teacher has 24 students who are randomly split into three groups of eight students each. The first group of eight students are taught beginning typing in a usual classroom; the second group of students spend the first six weeks in the classroom, but spend the remainder of the year typing at their own discretion and interest dictates; the third group of students remain in the regular classroom for 18 weeks and spend the remaining portion of the school year serving as teacher aides working directly with typing. Five minute timed typing tests are given to all three groups at intervals of twelve weeks. Results are recorded in gross words per minute.

Group 1

Student	12 Weeks	24 Weeks	36 Weeks
1	28	37	49
2	32	41	48
3	36	56	67
4	32	49	56
5	35	55	60
6	37	56	63
7	39	49	57
8	46	69	75

Group 2

Student	12 Weeks	24 Weeks	36 Weeks
9	29	36	35
10	47	65	76
11	32	39	41
12	37	48	52
13	32	35	34
14	34	52	61
15	32	37	39
16	36	46	62

Group 3

Student	12 Weeks	24 Weeks	36 Weeks
17	38	52	58
18	42	55	60
19	37	51	53
20	27	40	47
21	24	32	40
22	36	46	53
23	32	54	61
24	36	56	63

Test for trend, methods, and methods X trend.

CHAPTER FOURTEEN

OTHER APPROACHES TO DATA ANALYSIS

14.1 Other Regression Approaches

When completing the reading of a text, it is natural to ask, where are we at? It seems reasonable to answer the question just posed. As was briefly pointed out in Chapter One, several alternative approaches to data analysis could be made in a regression framework. One particular peculiarity of this text, in comparison to the others previously mentioned, is that an extremely limited mathematical background is assumed on the part of the reader. Further, a single computer program, likely to be available in most college and university computer centers, has been used. At this point, further readings in the regression area are suggested.

For the reader interested in applications to the field of education and educational psychology, Kelly, Beggs and McNeil (1969) should prove to be a readable text. A slight drawback to their approach is a necessity of the use of a different regression computer program than is commonly used; the complete documentation of the program is in their Appendix, however. Local debugging of the program does take a little effort, and some cooperation from the local computer center is necessary to fully implement Kelly, Beggs and McNeil's approach.

The presentation by Bottenberg and Ward (1963), which has been superseded to some degree by Ward and Jennings (1973), is an important contribution in the use of multiple linear regression. Both presentations use matrix algebra in the solutions they provide. From the point of view of a non-mathematician, their matrix usage is not excessive, and with some effort, their use of matrix algebra should be no barrier to the serious reader. A unique part of both these texts is that an attempt is made to use regression to solve questions stated in a natural language form. They use natural language questions to impose restrictions on the regression coefficients which result in restricted models as a natural consequence.

Mendenhall's (1968) presentation is in a somewhat different vein than those mentioned earlier in this chapter, although his approach also uses linear models in the regression solution to the analysis of variance situation. A particularly lucid chapter on the use of matrix algebra (Chapter Six) shows the least squares solution to an analysis of variance model.

A more typical use of regression is given by Draper and Smith (1966). They have an extensive presentation regarding several stepwise techniques. Their presentation is perhaps the most mathematically oriented of any of the texts mentioned here.

14.2 Other Approaches to Data Analysis in the Analysis of Variance

The approach of the present text has been to consider many of the problems encountered in a typical analysis of variance presentation, but from a regression approach. For the reader who is familiar with the more traditional approaches to topics in the analysis of covariance in such texts as Edwards (1972), Lindquist (1953), or Winer (1971), an appreciation of the regression approach seems most likely. In many ways, the problems considered in the present text parallel the problems given in a more conventional approach; the techniques given here are intended to greatly simplify the actual data analysis.

Some readers may be motivated to study an area called experimental design, which is perhaps best typified by Winer (1971), although the other two mentioned texts in this section have been prominently used. Other readers may be interested in an area called multivariate analysis. The use of multiple correlations can be thought of as a starting place for a multivariate analysis. Many additional techniques, such as cluster analysis, factor analysis, cannonical correlation, discriminant analysis, and the multivariate analysis of variance are typically presented. A monograph by Kendall (1965) is quite readable. Several texts have recently been written for the applications of multivariate analysis, including Cooley and Lohnes (1971), Tatsuoka (1971), Overall and Klett (1972) and Press (1972).

14.3 A Final Note on Computer Programs

As indicated throughout this text, to effect the solutions, only a multiple linear regression program is needed (except for setwise regression). The specific program used for the solutions in this text are from the IBM (1968) Scientific Subroutine Package, which is widely available.

On the other hand, other packages are quite attractive, such as the Statistical Package for the Social Sciences (SPSS; Nie, Bent and Hull, 1970), which include many applications of interest to the applied researcher. The SPSS package is an all inclusive set of programs that is sold commercially. Veldman (1967) presents several programs that can be directly implemented with a minimum of programming effort. Two journals, Behavioral Science and Educational and Psychological Measurement, regularly report newly written programs that are available from individual authors.

Additional regression programs are available in the Appendices of both Kelly, Beggs and McNeil (1969), and Ward and Jennings (1973) which relate directly to the approaches given respectively in each text.

A special interest group on multiple linear regression of the American Educational Research Association (AERA) has been active for the last several years. At the 1974 AERA Convention, the entire program of the special interest group was devoted to the various programs written by members of the group related to multiple linear regression. Descriptions of these programs and the presentations are given in an issue of Multiple Linear Regression Viewpoints, the organ of this special interest group.

TABLES

Table I Distribution of t for Given Probability Levels, computed by Alfred C. Lindem, Jr. on an IBM-370-135 computer system at the University of North Dakota.

Tables IIa and IIb The F Distribution (.01 and .05 Levels), computed by Alfred C. Lindem, Jr. on an IBM-370-135 computer system at the University of North Dakota.

Tables IIIa and IIIb Percentage Points of the Studentized Range (.01 and .05 Levels), Reproduced from H. L. Harter. Tables of range and studentized range. Annals of Mathematical Statistics, 1960, 31, 1122-1147, with permission of the author.

Tables IVa and IVb Percentage Points of Dunnett's Test (.01 and .05 Levels; One-tailed) and

Tables Va and Vb Percentage Points of Dunnett's Test (.01 and .05 Levels; Two-tailed), both reproduced from C. W. Dunnett, A multiple comparison procedure for comparing several treatments with a control. Journal of the American Statistical Association, 1955, 50, 1096-1121, and C. W. Dunnett, New tables for multiple comparisons with a control. Biometrics, 1964, 20, 482-491, with permission of the author.

For Tables IIIa, IIIb, IVa, IVb. Va and Vb, v refers to the degrees of freedom within (df_w).

For Tables IIIa and IIIb, r refers to the number of means in the range; for Tukey's test r thus is equal to the number of groups.

For Tables IVa, IVb, Va and Vb, k refers to the number of groups compared to the control (excluding the control).

TABLE I

DISTRIBUTION OF t FOR GIVEN PROBABILITY LEVELS

	Level of significance for one-tailed test				
	.05	.025	.01	.005	.0005
	Level of significance for two-tailed test				
	.10	.05	.02	.01	.001
df					
1	6.314	12.076	31.821	63.657	636.619
2	2.920	4.303	6.965	9.925	31.598
3	2.353	3.182	4.541	5.841	12.941
4	2.132	2.776	3.747	4.604	8.610
5	2.015	2.571	3.365	4.032	6.859
6	1.943	2.447	3.143	3.707	5.959
7	1.895	2.365	2.998	3.499	5.405
8	1.860	2.306	2.896	3.355	5.041
9	1.833	2.262	2.821	3.250	4.781
10	1.812	2.228	2.764	3.169	4.587
11	1.796	2.201	2.718	3.106	4.437
12	1.782	2.179	2.681	3.055	4.318
13	1.771	2.160	2.650	3.012	4.221
14	1.761	2.145	2.624	2.977	4.140
15	1.753	2.131	2.602	2.947	4.073
16	1.746	2.120	2.583	2.921	4.015
17	1.740	2.110	2.567	2.898	3.965
18	1.734	2.101	2.552	2.878	3.992
19	1.729	2.093	2.539	2.861	3.883
20	1.725	2.086	2.528	2.845	3.850
24	1.711	2.064	2.492	2.797	3.745
30	1.697	2.042	2.457	2.750	3.646
40	1.684	2.021	2.423	2.704	3.551
60	1.671	2.000	2.390	2.660	3.460
120	1.658	1.980	2.358	2.617	3.373
∞	1.645	1.960	2.326	2.576	3.291

TABLE IIa

THE F DISTRIBUTION (.05 LEVEL)

Degrees of freedom denominator	Degrees of Freedom for Numerator 1	2	3	4	5	6	7	8	9	10	20
1	161.4	199.5	215.7	224.6	230.2	234.0	236.8	238.9	240.5	241.9	248.0
2	18.51	19.00	19.16	19.25	19.30	19.33	19.35	19.37	19.38	19.40	19.45
3	10.13	9.55	9.28	9.12	9.01	8.94	8.89	8.85	8.81	8.79	8.66
4	7.71	6.94	6.59	6.39	6.26	6.16	6.09	6.04	6.00	5.96	5.80
5	6.61	5.79	5.41	5.19	5.05	4.95	4.88	4.82	4.78	4.74	4.56
6	5.99	5.14	4.76	4.53	4.39	4.28	4.21	4.15	4.10	4.06	3.87
7	5.59	4.74	4.35	4.12	3.97	3.87	3.79	3.73	3.68	3.63	3.44
8	5.32	4.46	4.07	3.84	3.69	3.58	3.50	3.44	3.39	3.34	3.15
9	5.12	4.26	3.86	3.63	3.48	3.37	3.29	3.23	3.18	3.13	2.93
10	4.96	4.10	3.71	3.48	3.33	3.22	3.14	3.07	3.02	2.97	2.77
11	4.84	3.98	3.59	3.36	3.20	3.09	3.01	2.95	2.90	2.86	2.65
12	4.75	3.89	3.49	3.26	3.11	3.00	2.92	2.85	2.80	2.76	2.54
13	4.67	3.81	3.41	3.18	3.03	2.92	2.83	2.77	2.71	2.67	2.46
14	4.60	3.74	3.34	3.11	2.96	2.85	2.76	2.70	2.65	2.60	2.39
15	4.54	3.68	3.29	3.06	2.90	2.79	2.70	2.64	2.59	2.55	2.33
16	4.49	3.63	3.24	3.01	2.85	2.74	2.66	2.59	2.54	2.49	2.28
17	4.45	3.59	3.20	2.96	2.81	2.70	2.61	2.55	2.49	2.45	2.23
18	4.41	3.55	3.16	2.93	2.77	2.66	2.58	2.51	2.46	2.41	2.19
19	4.38	3.52	3.13	2.90	2.74	2.63	2.54	2.48	2.42	2.38	2.16
20	4.25	3.49	3.10	2.87	2.71	2.60	2.52	2.45	2.40	2.35	2.12
30	4.17	3.32	2.92	2.69	2.53	2.42	2.34	2.27	2.21	2.16	1.93
40	4.08	3.23	2.84	2.61	2.45	2.34	2.25	2.18	2.12	2.07	1.84
60	4.00	3.15	2.76	2.52	2.37	2.25	2.17	2.10	2.04	1.99	1.75
120	3.92	3.07	2.68	2.44	2.29	2.17	2.08	2.01	1.95	1.90	1.65
∞	3.84	2.99	2.60	2.37	2.21	2.09	2.01	1.94	1.88	1.83	1.57

TABLE IIb

THE F DISTRIBUTION (.01 LEVEL)

degrees of freedom denominator	Degrees of Freedom for Numerator: 1	2	3	4	5	6	7	8	9	10	20
1	4052	4999.5	5403	5625	5764	5859	5928	5982	6022	6056	6209
2	98.5	99.00	99.17	99.25	99.30	99.33	99.36	99.37	99.39	99.40	99.45
3	34.12	30.82	29.46	28.71	28.24	27.91	27.67	27.49	27.35	27.23	26.69
4	21.20	18.00	16.69	15.98	15.52	15.21	14.98	14.80	14.66	14.55	14.02
5	16.26	13.27	12.06	11.39	10.97	10.67	10.45	10.27	10.15	10.05	9.55
6	13.74	10.92	9.78	9.15	8.75	8.45	8.26	8.10	7.98	7.87	7.39
7	12.25	9.55	8.45	7.85	8.45	7.19	7.00	6.84	6.71	6.62	6.15
8	11.26	8.65	7.59	7.01	6.63	6.37	6.19	6.03	5.91	5.82	5.36
9	10.56	8.02	6.99	6.42	6.06	5.80	5.62	5.47	5.35	5.26	4.80
10	10.04	7.56	6.55	5.99	5.64	5.39	5.21	5.06	4.95	4.85	4.41
11	9.65	7.20	6.22	5.67	5.32	5.07	4.88	4.74	4.63	4.54	4.01
12	9.33	6.93	5.95	5.41	5.06	4.82	4.65	4.50	4.39	4.30	3.86
13	9.07	6.70	5.74	5.21	4.86	4.62	4.44	4.30	4.19	4.10	3.66
14	8.86	6.51	5.56	5.04	4.69	4.46	4.28	4.14	4.03	3.94	3.51
15	8.68	6.36	5.42	4.89	4.56	4.32	4.14	4.00	3.89	3.80	3.36
16	8.53	6.23	5.29	4.77	4.44	4.20	4.03	3.89	3.78	3.69	3.26
17	8.40	6.11	5.18	4.67	4.34	4.10	3.93	3.79	3.68	3.59	3.16
18	8.29	6.01	5.09	4.58	4.25	4.01	3.84	3.71	3.60	3.51	3.08
19	8.18	5.93	5.01	4.50	4.17	3.94	3.77	3.63	3.52	3.43	3.00
20	8.10	5.85	4.94	4.43	4.10	3.87	3.71	3.56	3.45	3.37	2.94
30	7.56	5.39	4.51	4.02	3.70	3.47	3.30	3.17	3.06	2.98	2.55
40	7.31	5.18	4.31	3.83	3.51	3.29	3.12	2.99	2.88	2.80	2.37
60	7.08	4.98	4.13	3.65	3.34	3.12	2.95	2.82	2.72	2.63	2.20
120	6.84	4.78	3.94	3.47	3.17	2.95	2.79	2.65	2.56	2.47	2.03
∞	6.64	4.60	3.78	3.32	3.02	2.80	2.64	2.51	2.41	2.32	1.87

TABLE IIIa

PERCENTAGE POINTS OF THE STUDENTIZED RANGE
(.05 LEVEL)

v \ r	2	3	4	5	6	7	8	9	10	20
5	3.635	4.602	5.218	5.673	6.033	6.330	6.582	6.802	6.995	8.208
6	3.461	4.339	4.896	5.305	5.628	5.895	6.122	6.319	6.493	7.587
7	3.344	4.165	4.681	5.060	5.359	5.606	5.815	5.998	6.158	7.170
8	3.261	4.041	4.529	4.886	5.167	5.399	5.597	5.767	5.918	6.870
9	3.199	3.949	4.415	4.756	5.024	5.244	5.432	5.595	5.739	6.644
10	3.151	3.887	4.327	4.654	4.912	5.124	5.305	5.461	5.599	6.467
11	3.113	3.820	4.256	4.574	4.823	5.028	5.202	5.353	5.487	6.326
12	3.082	3.773	4.199	4.508	4.751	4.950	5.119	5.265	5.395	6.209
13	3.055	3.735	4.151	4.453	4.690	4.885	5.049	5.192	5.318	6.112
14	3.033	3.702	4.111	4.407	4.639	4.829	4.990	5.131	5.254	6.029
15	3.014	3.674	4.076	4.367	4.595	4.782	5.940	5.077	5.198	5.958
16	2.998	3.649	4.046	4.333	4.557	4.741	4.897	5.031	5.150	5.897
17	2.984	3.628	4.020	4.303	4.524	4.705	4.858	4.991	5.108	5.842
18	2.971	3.609	3.997	4.277	4.495	4.673	4.824	4.956	5.071	5.794
19	2.960	3.593	3.977	4.253	4.469	4.645	4.794	4.924	5.038	5.752
20	2.950	3.578	3.958	4.232	4.445	4.620	4.768	4.896	5.008	5.714
30	2.888	3.486	3.845	4.102	4.302	4.464	4.602	4.720	4.824	5.475
40	2.858	3.442	3.791	4.039	4.232	4.389	4.521	4.635	4.735	5.358
60	2.929	3.399	3.737	3.977	4.163	4.314	4.441	4.550	4.646	5.241
120	2.800	3.356	3.685	3.917	4.096	4.241	4.363	4.468	4.560	5.126
∞	2.772	3.314	3.633	3.858	4.030	4.170	4.286	4.387	4.474	5.012

TABLE IIIb

PERCENTAGE POINTS OF THE STUDENTIZED RANGE
(.01 LEVEL)

v \ r	2	3	4	5	6	7	8	9	10	20
5	5.702	6.976	7.804	8.421	8.913	9.321	9.669	9.972	10.24	11.93
6	5.243	6.331	7.033	7.556	7.973	8.318	8.613	8.869	9.097	10.54
7	4.949	5.919	6.543	7.005	7.373	7.679	7.939	8.166	8.368	9.646
8	4.746	5.635	6.204	6.625	6.960	7.237	7.474	7.681	7.863	9.027
9	4.596	5.428	5.957	6.348	6.658	6.915	7.134	7.325	7.495	8.573
10	4.482	5.270	5.769	6.136	6.428	6.669	6.875	7.005	7.213	8.226
11	4.392	5.146	5.621	5.970	6.247	6.476	6.672	6.842	6.992	7.952
12	4.320	5.146	5.502	5.836	6.101	6.321	6.507	6.670	6.814	7.731
13	4.260	4.964	5.404	5.727	5.981	6.192	6.327	6.528	6.667	7.548
14	4.210	4.895	5.322	5.634	5.881	6.085	6.258	6.409	6.543	7.395
15	4.168	4.836	5.252	5.556	5.796	5.994	6.162	6.309	6.439	7.264
16	4.131	4.786	5.192	5.489	5.722	5.915	6.079	6.222	6.349	7.152
17	4.099	4.742	5.140	5.430	5.659	5.847	6.007	6.147	6.270	7.053
18	4.071	4.703	5.094	5.379	5.603	5.788	5.944	6.081	6.201	6.968
19	4.046	4.670	5.054	5.334	5.554	5.735	5.889	6.022	6.141	6.891
20	4.024	4.639	5.018	5.294	5.510	5.688	5.839	5.970	6.087	6.823
30	3.889	4.455	4.799	5.048	5.242	5.401	5.536	5.653	5.756	6.407
40	3.825	4.367	4.696	4.931	5.114	5.265	5.392	5.502	5.599	6.209
60	3.762	4.282	4.595	4.818	4.991	5.133	5.253	5.356	5.447	6.015
120	3.702	4.200	4.497	4.709	4.872	5.005	5.118	5.214	5.299	5.827
∞	3.643	4.120	4.403	4.603	4.757	4.882	4.987	5.078	5.157	5.645

TABLE IVa

PERCENTAGE POINTS OF DUNNETT'S TEST
(.05 LEVEL)

One-tailed

v \ k	1	2	3	4	5	6	7	8	9
5	2.02	2.44	2.68	2.85	2.98	3.08	3.16	3.24	3.30
6	1.94	2.34	2.56	2.71	2.83	2.92	3.00	3.07	3.12
7	1.89	2.27	2.48	2.62	2.73	2.82	2.89	2.95	3.01
8	1.86	2.22	2.42	2.55	2.66	2.74	2.81	2.87	2.92
9	1.83	2.18	2.37	2.50	2.60	2.68	2.75	2.81	2.86
10	1.81	2.15	2.34	2.47	2.56	2.64	2.70	2.76	2.81
11	1.80	2.13	2.31	2.44	2.53	2.60	2.67	2.72	2.77
12	1.78	2.11	2.29	2.41	2.50	2.58	2.64	2.69	2.74
13	1.77	2.09	2.27	2.39	2.48	2.55	2.61	2.66	2.71
14	1.76	2.08	2.25	2.37	2.46	2.53	2.59	2.64	2.69
15	1.75	2.07	2.24	2.36	2.44	2.51	2.57	2.62	2.67
16	1.75	2.06	2.23	2.34	2.43	2.50	2.56	2.61	2.65
17	1.74	2.05	2.22	2.33	2.42	2.49	2.54	2.59	2.64
18	1.73	2.04	2.21	2.32	2.41	2.48	2.53	2.58	2.62
19	1.73	2.03	2.20	2.31	2.40	2.47	2.52	2.57	2.61
20	1.72	2.03	2.19	2.30	2.39	2.46	2.51	2.56	2.60
30	1.70	1.99	2.15	2.25	2.33	2.40	2.45	2.50	2.54
40	1.68	1.97	2.13	2.23	2.31	2.37	2.42	2.47	2.51
60	1.67	1.95	2.10	2.21	2.28	2.35	2.39	2.44	2.48
120	1.66	1.93	2.08	2.18	2.26	2.32	2.37	2.41	2.45
∞	1.64	1.92	2.06	2.16	2.23	2.29	2.34	2.38	2.42

TABLE IVb

PERCENTAGE POINTS OF DUNNETT'S TEST
(.01 LEVEL)

One-tailed

v \ k	1	2	3	4	5	6	7	8	9
5	3.37	3.90	4.21	4.43	4.60	4.73	4.85	4.94	5.03
6	3.14	3.61	3.88	4.07	4.21	4.33	4.43	4.51	4.59
7	3.00	3.42	3.66	3.83	3.96	4.07	4.15	4.23	4.30
8	2.90	3.29	3.51	3.67	3.79	3.88	3.96	4.03	4.09
9	2.82	3.19	3.40	3.55	3.66	3.75	3.82	3.89	3.94
10	2.76	3.11	3.31	3.45	3.56	3.64	3.71	3.78	3.83
11	2.72	3.06	3.25	3.38	3.48	3.56	3.63	3.69	3.74
12	2.68	3.01	3.19	3.32	3.42	3.50	3.56	3.62	3.67
13	2.65	2.97	3.15	3.27	3.37	3.44	3.51	3.56	3.61
14	2.62	2.94	3.11	3.23	3.32	3.40	3.46	3.51	3.56
15	2.60	2.91	3.08	3.20	3.29	3.36	3.42	3.47	3.52
16	2.58	2.88	3.05	3.17	3.26	3.33	3.39	3.44	3.48
17	2.57	2.86	3.03	3.14	3.23	3.30	3.36	3.41	3.45
18	2.55	2.84	3.01	3.12	3.21	3.27	3.33	3.38	3.42
19	2.54	2.83	2.99	3.10	3.18	3.25	3.31	3.36	3.40
20	2.53	2.81	2.97	3.08	2.17	3.23	3.29	3.34	3.38
30	2.46	2.72	2.87	2.97	3.05	3.11	3.16	3.21	3.24
40	2.42	2.68	2.82	2.92	2.99	3.05	3.10	3.14	3.18
60	2.39	2.64	2.78	2.87	2.94	3.00	3.04	3.08	3.12
120	2.36	2.60	2.73	2.82	2.89	2.94	2.99	3.03	3.06
∞	2.33	2.56	2.68	2.77	2.84	2.89	2.93	2.97	3.00

TABLE Va

PERCENTAGE POINTS OF DUNNETT'S TEST
(.05 LEVEL)

Two-tailed

v \ k	1	2	3	4	5	6	7	8	9
5	2.57	3.03	3.29	3.48	3.62	3.73	3.82	3.90	3.97
6	2.45	2.86	3.10	3.26	3.39	3.49	3.57	3.64	3.71
7	2.36	2.75	2.97	3.12	3.24	3.33	3.41	3.47	3.53
8	2.31	2.67	2.88	3.02	3.13	3.22	3.29	3.5	3.41
9	2.26	2.61	2.81	2.95	3.05	3.14	3.20	3.26	3.32
10	2.23	2.57	2.76	2.89	2.99	3.07	3.14	3.19	3.24
11	2.20	2.53	2.72	2.84	2.94	3.02	3.08	3.14	3.19
12	2.18	2.50	2.68	2.81	2.90	2.98	3.04	3.09	3.14
13	2.16	2.48	2.65	2.78	2.87	2.94	3.00	3.06	3.10
14	2.14	2.46	2.63	2.75	2.84	2.91	2.97	3.02	3.07
15	2.13	2.44	2.61	2.73	2.82	2.89	2.95	3.00	3.04
16	2.12	2.42	2.59	2.71	2.80	2.87	2.92	2.97	3.02
17	2.11	2.41	2.58	2.69	2.78	2.85	2.90	2.95	3.00
18	2.10	2.40	2.56	2.68	2.76	2.83	2.89	2.94	2.98
19	2.09	2.39	2.55	2.66	2.75	2.81	2.87	2.92	2.96
20	2.09	2.38	2.54	2.65	2.73	2.80	2.86	2.90	2.95
30	2.04	2.32	2.47	2.58	2.66	2.72	2.77	2.82	2.86
40	2.02	2.29	2.44	2.54	2.62	2.68	2.73	2.77	2.81
60	2.00	2.27	2.41	2.51	2.58	2.64	2.69	2.73	2.77
120	1.98	2.24	2.38	2.47	2.55	2.60	2.65	2.69	2.73
∞	1.96	2.21	2.35	2.44	2.51	2.57	2.61	2.65	2.69

TABLE Vb

PERCENTAGE POINTS OF DUNNETT'S TEST
(.01 LEVEL)

Two-tailed

v \ k	1	2	3	4	5	6	7	8	9
5	4.03	4.63	4.98	5.22	5.41	5.56	5.69	5.80	5.89
6	3.71	4.21	4.51	4.71	4.87	5.00	5.10	5.20	5.28
7	3.50	3.95	4.21	4.39	4.53	4.64	4.74	4.82	4.89
8	3.36	3.77	4.00	4.17	4.29	4.40	4.48	4.56	4.62
9	3.25	3.63	3.85	4.01	4.12	4.22	4.30	4.37	4.43
10	3.17	3.53	3.74	3.88	3.99	4.08	4.16	4.22	4.28
11	3.11	3.45	3.65	3.79	3.89	3.98	4.05	4.11	4.16
12	3.05	3.39	3.58	3.71	3.81	3.89	3.96	4.02	4.07
13	3.01	3.33	3.52	3.65	3.74	3.82	3.89	3.94	3.99
14	2.98	3.29	3.47	3.59	3.69	3.76	3.83	3.88	3.93
15	2.95	3.25	3.43	3.55	3.64	3.71	3.78	3.83	3.88
16	2.92	3.22	3.39	3.51	3.60	3.67	3.73	3.78	3.83
17	2.90	3.19	3.36	3.47	3.56	3.63	3.69	3.74	3.79
18	2.88	3.17	3.33	3.44	3.53	3.60	3.66	3.71	3.75
19	2.86	3.15	3.31	3.42	3.50	3.57	3.63	3.68	3.72
20	2.85	3.13	3.29	3.40	3.48	3.55	3.60	3.65	3.69
30	2.75	3.01	3.15	3.25	3.33	3.39	3.44	3.49	3.52
40	2.70	2.95	3.09	3.19	3.26	3.32	3.37	3.41	3.44
60	2.66	2.90	3.03	3.12	3.19	3.25	3.29	3.33	3.37
120	2.62	2.85	2.97	3.06	3.12	3.18	3.22	3.26	3.29
∞	2.58	2.79	2.92	3.00	3.06	3.11	3.15	3.19	3.22

REFERENCES

Anderson, R. L., and Bancroft, T. A. Statistical theory in research. New York: McGraw-Hill, 1952.

Bleeker, R., and Kelly, C. A correlational study between the ITPA and the PPVT. Unpublished paper, The University of North Dakota, 1971.

Bottenberg, R. A., and Ward, J. H. Applied multiple linear regression. Lackland Air Force Base, Texas: Personnel Research Laboratory PRL-TDR-63-6, 1963.

Cohen, J. Multiple regression as a general data-analytic system. Psychological Bulletin, 1968, 70, 426-443.

Cooley, W. W., and Lohnes, P. R. Multivariate Data Analysis. New York: Wiley, 1971.

Creager, J. A. Orthogonal and nonorthogonal methods for partitioning regression variance. American Educational Research Journal, 1971, 8, 671-676.

Darlington, R. B. Multiple regression in psychological research and practice. Psychological Bulletin, 1968, 69, 161-182.

Dayton, C. M. The t-test: parametric or nonparamatric. Paper presented at the American Educational Research Association Convention, February 16, 1967.

Draper, N., and Smith, H. Applied Regression Analysis. New York: Wiley, 1966.

DuBois, P. H. Multivariate correlational analysis. New York: Harper and Row, 1957.

DuBois, P. H. Correlational analysis in training research, in DuBois, P. H., and Mayo, G. D. Research strategies for evaluating training. Chicago: Rand McNally, 1970.

Duncan, D. B. Multiple range and multiple F tests. Biometrics, 1955, 11, 1-42.

Dunn, O. J. Multiple comparisons among means. Journal of the American Statistical Association, 1961, 56: 52-64.

Dunnett, C. W. A multiple comparison procedure for comparing several treatments with a control. Journal of the American Statistical Association, 1955, 50: 1096-1121.

Dunnett, C. W. New tables for multiple comparisons with a control. Biometrics, 1964, 20, 482-491.

Edwards, A. L. Experimental Design in Psychological Research. 4th Ed. New York: Holt, Rinehart and Winston, 1972.

Glass, G. V., and Stanley, J. C. Statistical Methods in Education and Psychology. Englewood Cliffs, New Jersey: Prentice-Hall, 1970.

Grooters, L. L. A study of program offerings and factors affecting instructional salary costs in major curricula at the four state colleges in North Dakota. Unpublished doctoral dissertation, The University of North Dakota, 1971.

Halldorson, M. H. An iterative multiple regression technique for the factorial analysis of variance with unequal and disproportional cell frequencies. Doctoral dissertation, The University of Northern Colorado, 1969.

IBM, System/360 scientific subroutine package (360A-CM-03X) version III programmers manual. White Plains, New York: IBM Technical Publications Department, 1968.

Jennings, E. Fixed effects analysis of variance by regression analysis. Multivariate Behavioral Research, 1967, 2, 95-108.

Jennings, E. Linear models underlying the analysis of covariance, residual gain scores and raw gain scores. Multiple Linear Regression Viewpoints, 1972, 3, 17-24.

Jordan, T. E. Curvilinearity within early developmental variables. Presented at the American Educational Research Association Convention, New York, 1971.

Kelly, F. J., Beggs, D. L., and McNeil, K. A. Multiple regression approach. Carbondale, Ill.: Southern Illinois University Press, 1969.

Keuls, M. The use of studentized range in connection with an analysis of variance. Euphytica, 1952, 1, 112-122.

Lindquist, E. F. Design and analysis of experiments in psychology and education. Boston: Houghton Mifflin Company, 1953.

Maresh, R. An analysis of the effects of vertical grade groups on reading achievement and attitudes in elementary schools. Unpublished doctoral dissertation, The University of North Dakota.

Mendenhall, W. The design and analysis of experiments. Belmont, California: Wadsworth, 1968.

Myers, J. L. Fundamentals of experimental design. Boston: Allyn and Bacon, 1966.

Newman, D. The distribution of range in samples from a normal population, expressed in terms of an independent estimate of standard deviation. Biometrika, 1939, 31, 20-30.

Nie, N. H., Bent, D. H., & Hull, C. H. Statistical package for the social sciences. New York: McGraw-Hill, 1970.

Norton, D. W. An empirical investigation of some effects of non-normality and heterogeneity on the F-distribution. Unpublished doctoral dissertation, The State University of Iowa, 1952.

Overall, J. E., and Klett, C. J. Applied multivariate analysis. New York: McGraw-Hill, 1972.

Overall, J. E., and Spiegle, D. K. Concerning least squares analysis of experimental data. Psychological Bulletin, 1969, 72, 311-322.

Paluck, C. Correlations of the Kuhlman-Anderson I.Q. test. Unpublished paper, The University of North Dakota, 1968.

Press, S. J. Applied multivariate analysis. New York: McGraw-Hill, 1972.

Randolph, N., and Howe, W. Self enhancing education. Palo Alto, Calif.: Educational Development Corporation, 1966.

Rao, C. R. Linear statistical inference and its applications. New York: Wiley, 1965.

Ryan, T. A. Multiple comparisons in psychological research. Psychological Bulletin, 1959, 56, 26-47.
Ryan, T. A. Significance tests for multiple comparisons of proportions, variance, and other statistics. Psychological Bulletin, 1969, 57, 318-328.
Scheffé, H. A method for judging all contrasts in the analysis of variance. Biometrika, 1953, 40, 87-104.
Scheffé, H. The analysis of variance. New York: John Wiley & Sons, 1959.
Schmid, J. Research design with multiple regression. Dittoed, The University of Northern Colorado, 1967.
Siegel, S. Nonparametric statistics for the behavioral sciences. New York: McGraw-Hill, 1956.
Snedecor, G. W., and Cox, G. M. Disproportionate subclass numbers in tables of multiple classification. Iowa State College Agricultural Experiment Station Bulletin, 1935.
Steinhorst, R. K., and Miller, C. D. Disproportionality of cell frequencies in psychological and educational experiments involving multiple classification. Educational and Psychological Measurement, 1969, 29, 799-811.
Tatsuoka, M. M. Multivariate Analysis. New York: John Wiley and Sons, 1971.
Tukey, J. W. Causation, regression and path analysis. In Kemphorne, O. (Ed.) Statistics and mathematics in biology. Ames, Iowa: Iowa State College Press, 1954.
Veldman, D. J. Fortran programming for the behavioral sciences. New York: Holt, Rinehart and Winston, 1967.
Walker, H. M., and Lev, J. Statistical inference. New York: Holt, Rinehart and Winston, 1953.
Ward, J. H. Partitioning of variance and contribution or importance of a variable: a visit to a graduate seminar. American Educational Research Journal, 1969, 467-474.
Ward, J. H., and Hook, M. E. Use of regression analysis and electronic computers in the prediction of coronary artery disease. Behavioral Science, 1962, 7, 120-126.
Ward, J. H., and Jennings, E. Introduction to Linear Models. Englewood Cliffs, N. J.: Prentice-Hall, 1973.
Werts, C. E. The partitioning of variance in school effects studies: a reconsideration. American Educational Research Journal, 1970, 7, 127-132.
Williams, J. D. Multiple comparisons in a regression approach. Psychological Reports, 1972a, 30, 639-647.
Williams, J. D. Two way fixed effects analysis of variance with disproportional cell frequencies. Multivariate Behavioral Research, 1972b, 7, 67-83.
Williams, J. D. Human Awareness through Self Enhancing Education: The Third Year Report. Grand Forks, N.D. Public Schools, 1973.
Williams, J. D., and Buzahora, R. G. An empirical comparison of the analysis of covariance and the residual gain analysis. Multiple Linear Regression Viewpoints, 1973 (in press).

Williams, J. D., Harlow, S. D., & Gab, D. A Longitudinal Study Examining Prediction of Doctoral Success: Grade Point Average as Criterion, or Graduation vs. Non-Graduation as Criterion. Journal of Educational Research, 1970, 64, 161-164.

Williams, J. D., Harlow, S. D., & Houston, S. R. Action research for the classroom teacher. Dubuque, Iowa: Kendall/Hunt, 1969.

Williams, J. D., and Lindem, A. C. Setwise regression analysis--A stepwise procedure for sets of variables. Educational and Psychological Measurement, 1971, 31, 747-778.

Williams, J. D., and Lindem, A. C. Analysis of covariance with multiple covariates. Educational and Psychological Measurement, 1972, 32, 815-816.

Winer, B. J. Statistical principles in experimental design. 2nd Ed. New York: McGraw-Hill, 1971.